Take Rapid Action:

Get Productive, Motivated, & Energized; Stop Overthinking & Procrastinating [Second Edition]

By Patrick King
Social Interaction and Conversation Coach at
www.PatrickKingConsulting.com

Table of Contents

Table of Contents 5
Chapter 1. Stop Overthinking..................... 7
   Follow the Ostrich's Lead 11
   The Premortem Analysis 16
   The Don't-Do List................................... 22
   Accept the Uncertainty of Action 28

Chapter 2. Err on the Side of Action 37
   Get a Little Uncomfortable 38
   Tiny Steps 45
   The 40-70 Rule....................................... 51
   Beat Indecision 55
   Limit Consumption for More Production... 65

Chapter 3. The Take-Action Mindset 79
   Motivation Follows Action 81
   No More "Zero Days" 85
   Solution Versus Problem Mindset..... 90
   Intentions Versus Actions 96
   Important Versus Urgent 102

Chapter 4. Maximize Momentum......... 117
  Banish Your Excuses 118
  Temptation Bundling............................ 127
  Improve Your Environment 130
  The If-Then Technique......................... 135
  Single-tasking.. 137
  25 Minutes at a Time............................ 144

Chapter 5. Beating Procrastination ... 157
  9 Subscales of Failure 163
  Task Versus Ego Orientation............. 180

Cheat Sheet.. 195

Chapter 1. Stop Overthinking

Act or accept. - Anonymous

In light of the theme of this book, I opted to skip the introduction and get right to the meat of the matter so you can, of course, take action more rapidly.

Overthinking is the antithesis of springing into action, and the place we start when we think about taking action. Either we do what's necessary, or we engage in the mental hamster wheel that keeps us stuck in place = no action. Thinking too much is the mortal enemy of getting started and can seduce you into mistakenly believing that you've done your duty because it can sometimes be so tiring = no action. Most often, it occurs when we fail to draw a distinction between the proper amount of due diligence and obsessive fixation = no action.

Suppose you want to start a business and you've been dreaming about it for months. You have all the details planned in your head, and the list of questions you need answers to only seems to grow without ever shrinking.

What if everything fails? What if you lose all your money? What if not a single person buys your product? What kind of forks should you have in the company cafeteria? How will you deal with your taxes? What type of animal will the company mascot be?

Now, some of these are important questions. But some are not, especially not at the current moment, when they have no relevance or urgency to the greater task at hand. Nonetheless, you find yourself wasting away precious hours tossing and turning in bed while analyzing everything at three a.m. Your mind is going a mile a minute because you are playing out all the possible scenarios in your head. You can't seem to shut off your brain even when you are physically exhausted. And yet, you are zero steps closer to turning your thoughts into a reality.

You tell yourself to stop thinking about it and get into motion. But you simply can't stop thinking about the what-ifs. You're tired, you lose sleep, and you're consumed by distracting thoughts—some fixated on failure and problems as a reflection of your insecurities, and some that don't matter at all but are disguised as important.

Instead of taking action, you feel paralyzed by your planning. Things have to go well, and you can't risk any type of failure, so you keep forecasting and trying to predict the future. There are just too many thoughts swirling around your head, and since you feel so overwhelmed, it's like you've lost even before you've started, and your business is never begun.

To a certain extent, overthinking about problems in particular is important because it helps you navigate everyday life. As a human being, you are hardwired to worry about what can go wrong; danger used to be lurking behind every bush, after all. This tendency allows you to think of all possible scenarios and prepare to survive. This keeps you out of trouble and safe more often than not. In moderation, it's an admirable trait. But that's not why you're reading this book.

This type of overactive, hyperactive mental chatter has a considerable downside: you can't *think* and *do* at the same time. Perhaps for the brain, a lack of action is truly the safest way to live, but it ignores that *doing* is the only thing we are measured by in this world. Your overactive mind will hold you back from everything, from the easiest tasks to calculated risks. At the basic level, overthinking can make you tired, scared, and stuck in life. In more extreme cases, overthinking can cause anxiety and shut you out completely from your goals, desires, and beliefs. As you'll read here, our brains are quite adept at sabotaging our best intentions.

Is it just as easy to quiet your mind as stepping into a soundproof room? Well, no. That's a tough habit to crack. But at the very least, there are ways to redirect that extra energy you use to run in place and avoid taking a single step forward. These methods start with zeroing in on what you spend your overthinking quota on, and how to cut it shorter.

Follow the Ostrich's Lead

According to a popular myth, ostriches instinctively bury their heads in the sand when they sense trouble because it makes them feel safer. It is supposedly a defense mechanism akin to the saying, "Out of sight, out of mind." In reality, these beautiful birds don't really live that way. As fast animals possessing enormously powerful legs, they are better off trying to outrun trouble or stomp it into submission with said legs.

In the finance world, the Ostrich Theory refers to how investors will simply avoid looking at stocks and related information if they know there is a chance that their numbers are down. It refers to the human tendency to avoid confirming danger in order to feel safe and not affirm the worst. It appears that psychologically, a sense of ignorance is preferable to a tangible negative.

It may not make logical sense, but it sure feels good to our sense of comfort. It allows you to deny your worst feelings because you don't know for sure that the negative consequence exists. Without knowing the reality of the situation, you don't have to face it, even if you have a strong notion it's lurking just around the corner.

People typically demonstrate this behavior when they don't want to confront a harsh truth or unpleasant situation. For instance, if you have a feeling that you've gained weight, then despite your doctor telling you that you're obese, you may avoid all mirrors and scales for the time being. What you don't know won't hurt you, right? The Ostrich Theory plays on the protective instincts of human nature.

While most rightfully view the Ostrich Theory as something negative, it can actually be beneficial to our overarching goal of prioritizing action over thinking. How exactly is that?

A large aspect of overthinking focuses on fears and insecurities. We're terrified of judgment, rejection, or flat-out failure, so having our heads in the sand and not being constantly bombarded by these worst-case scenarios can help us make a leap instead of analyzing every fearful possibility. It might seem that I'm encouraging you to ignore important signs that can potentially teach you a lot—that's definitely not the case. The point I'm making is that most of the negative chatter is indeed useless, and you would be better served completely ignoring these thoughts. They only serve to implant an extraneous "what if?" in your head and raise your alarms.

When you overthink, you have the tendency to treat everything as urgent and important. In fact, sometimes that is what we subconsciously want to do in order to avoid action. However, it's far from reality, so when you can occasionally engage in the Ostrich Theory and cut off a certain percentage of your negative chatter, the more likely the chance (however small) that you'll take action.

It comes down to *willful ignorance*—something that is also typically seen as negative. Keep yourself unaware of unnecessary information that will only throw off your focus, no matter if it is positive or negative. Willful ignorance is when you are able to distinguish what really matters at the moment and tune out everything else.

The way to put the Ostrich Theory into action is to occasionally bury your head in the sand. Intentionally limit the amount of information you intake. For instance, purposefully detox from the news or stay away from social media. Consider only the complaints or opinions of a select few whom you proactively seek out. Don't check your texts or e-mails before you take the first step. Set an upper limit for how many articles you will read concerning a potential problem. Block out certain concerns by diminishing returns (if you already know about a potential problem, you already know about it!), by source (we all have those negative influences in our lives), immediacy (some things simply don't matter at the moment; if you are at step four then why worry about step fifteen?), or category (what you are worried about may not actually impact the end goal or purpose).

Going back to the business example from earlier, you can stop researching your competitors and how much they make. Willful ignorance may be detrimental by itself, but when you pair it with obsessive overthinking and procrastination, it can balance you out. Other businesses may not matter for the time being, when you should be focused on how to simply get your first client, instead of going up against an entrenched competitor.

It might feel like something is falling through the cracks if you don't obsessively overthink and research, but the truth is, you'll learn far more from taking the first step and gaining firsthand experience rather than planning from the sidelines. As it turns out, experience is truly the best teacher and planner. Use the Ostrich Theory to try to get to that step sooner rather than later. So strap on a pair of blinders, limit your vision to only your immediate concerns, and walk forward step by step.

The Premortem Analysis

If you truly can't stomach the thought of starting something without analyzing a complete plan, you can try making a *premortem analysis*. Think of it as a more strategic way of overthinking that cuts down on the length that we so desire. The premortem analysis was invented by psychologist Gary Klein, and works by looking ahead to scenarios where you have failed, and working backward to find causes, weaknesses, threats, and flaws. The more well-known postmortem analysis looks at a situation, analyzes what went wrong, and finds a solution *after* the fact—the premortem attempts to do this *before* the fact to avoid those flaws. This creates a laser focus for your mental chatter, instead of being overwhelmed with everything and anything.

Now, this type of analysis has value for its own sake.

Instead of trying to plan everything you need for success, change your approach and plan what to do to avoid failure. Focus on avoiding one type of outcome, as opposed to seeking another out. This type of analysis can help you plan better and more effectively for the long term, and it forces you to look at your strategies from a different perspective. It's simple and can help avoid potential pitfalls in any endeavor, which is what we are typically most afraid of. Because you allow yourself to fail on paper, you are able to highlight possible problems that you might've otherwise missed because you were thinking of so many things.

How does this aid with taking action? The premortem analysis only gives you one scenario or set of variables to think about: failure. It's easier to think in an organized manner when you only have to imagine one outcome. It cuts all the other chatter out of your mind and streamlines your thoughts. This type of analysis spotlights the most important factor and organizes just a few scenarios to think through.

Imagine the failure, brainstorm some potential causes, see how you can address them (or if you can at all), and then jump. This approach to action strikes a large contrast with the type of unorganized and scattered thought that typically holds you back. Of course, this is only if you can actually use the premortem analysis to *replace* your other mental chatter, instead of adding it to your checklist of things to fret about. That's the tough step, but hopefully u this analysis once or twice will show you how much information it can yield so you can start to forego other thoughts.

Let's take an example of imagining how a hypothetical business will fail. Imagine the year is 2023 and your organic baby food business just went bankrupt. Let's assume you lost money every year since 2021. If you were to make a hypothesis, what are the causes of a future failure? You probably know what to focus your efforts on. So what happened? What went wrong? Zoom in on the possible causes of failure based on what you're worried about right now. Was it inadequate market research? Was there ineffective communication in your organization? Was it a competitor? Margins that were too thin to begin with?

Ask what you can do with only those four factors at the current moment. If the answer is nothing, which is likely, make a note for later, and then jump into action. After all, the thing you are most worried about is failure, so in theory, you've just addressed your greatest threats. Four clear threads of thought beats ten disorganized ones. Once you thoroughly think about how to avoid failure, what's left other than to make an attempt to prove yourself right or wrong?

Engage only in your premortem analysis and resist planning paralysis. Gathering more information than you absolutely need, conducting multiple analyses of different ways to achieve something, combing over minute and usually unnecessary details, debating back and forth in your own head about multiple scenarios—all of these actions are used as something that will postpone your taking action. After all, it's easier to *plan* than to *do*.

Planning in itself is a comfort zone, and not only because you can do it from a couch. To do something, you have to get outside and risk a certain vulnerability. So it's always easier to keep planning, because technically, it's useful to your task. You can lead yourself to believe you're being productive toward your overall goal. Keep in mind that over-planning is an often redundant process that people hide behind.

Finally, the premortem forces you to think only in terms of pertinent knowledge as opposed to *just in case* knowledge. *Just in case* knowledge is information that you're not sure you'll need, but you want to overthink on *just in case* an improbable and unlikely situation comes to pass. You might understand this better in the case of an extensive wardrobe, packed with a pink feathered scarf and a pair of purple military fatigue sweatpants just in case you happen to attend an "eccentric neon" theme night somewhere. At some point, you'll likely realize that what you are preparing for *just in case* is really never to occur.

As has been mentioned, being prepared is an admirable trait, but this book is aimed at kicking us into gear more frequently and consistently. To do so, you must risk feeling slightly less prepared by understanding that a lot of what you're using to hold yourself back from action is not important, and is in fact *just in case*-based knowledge that will ultimately be useless.

Plutarch once famously wrote, "Spartans do not ask how many are the enemy, but where are they." The meaning? The Spartans would be there to fight any enemy regardless of how many there were, and additional information wouldn't change their tactics in any way. The number was not important, so they only gathered the minimum information they needed and went forth with action.

The Don't-Do List

Sometimes when we're overthinking, it's because we can't choose what to first turn our attention to. Too many things have the potential to command our focus, and sometimes we can't differentiate between what we should avoid and what actually deserves our attention. We also may feel that everything is urgent and important. Thus, the focus of this section is to make crystal clear what you should be avoiding. It's similar to the Ostrich Theory and willful ignorance, in that you need to be intentional about what you feel like you are letting go of. In reality, you aren't letting go—you're streamlining.

Now, everyone knows the value of the to-do list. No doubt you've stumbled across tips elsewhere about using a to-do list to increase productivity and your ability to take action.

My point is that everyone inherently *kind of* knows what they should be doing and when they need to do it by. The act of writing it down just helps remind them and keep them accountable. This makes them more likely to do what they know they should be doing—more than if they didn't have such a list.

But not everyone knows what they *shouldn't* be doing. Each day, we're faced with trying to figure out what will create the biggest impact for us—and sometimes we spend time we don't have trying to make this choice. Again, we all know the obvious evils to avoid when trying to upgrade productivity: social media, goofing around on the internet, watching *The Bachelorette* while trying to work, or learning to play the flute while reading.

It can be difficult to distinguish between real tasks and useless tasks, and it will require some hard thought on your part. If you're lucky, you may find that you put almost everything onto your don't-do list, leaving an obvious path for you to take action.

You need to fill your don't-do list with tasks that will sneakily steal your time and undermine your goals. These are tasks that (1) are insignificant, (2) are a poor use of your time, (3) don't help your bottom line or end purpose, and (4) have a serious case of diminishing returns the more you work on them. If you continuously waste your time on these tasks, your real priorities will fall by the wayside.

I've identified three general types of tasks to put on your don't-do list:

First, tasks that are priorities, but you can't do anything about them at present because of external circumstances.

These are tasks that are important in one or many ways, but are waiting for feedback from others or for underlying tasks to be completed first. Put these on your don't-do list because there is literally nothing you can do about them!

Don't spend your mental energy thinking about them. They'll still be there when you hear back from those other people. Just note that you are waiting to hear back from someone else and the date on which you need to follow up if you haven't heard back. Then push these out of your mind, because they're on someone else's to-do list, not yours. The ball is in someone else's court, for better or worse.

Second are tasks that don't add value as far as your main goals and projects are concerned.

There are many small items that don't add to your bottom line, and often, these are trivial things—busywork. Do they really require your time? For that matter, are they *worth* your time? These tasks are just wasted motion for the sake of motion and don't really matter in the big picture. This is where we come to differentiating between aimless motion and actual intentional action. They are easily disguised as each other, right down to the fact that they both feel good to engage in. However, one delivers an outcome that you want (action), and the other is something that doesn't accomplish anything in the end (motion). You can spend a lot of time investigating gyms and researching workout routines, but if you never step foot inside of one, that's a whole lot of wasted motion running on a hamster wheel.

So you should spend your time on bigger tasks that speak to your overall goals and not myopic, trivial tasks. Often, these are useless tasks disguised as important ones, such as selecting the paint color for the bike shed in the parking lot of the nuclear power plant you are building.

Third, include tasks that are current and ongoing, but will not benefit from additional work or attention paid to them.

These tasks suffer from diminishing returns.

These projects are just a waste of energy because while they can still stand to improve (and is there anything that can't?), the amount of likely improvement will either not make a difference in the overall outcome or success, or will take a disproportionate amount of time and effort without making a significant dent.

For all intents and purposes, these tasks should be considered *done*. Don't waste your time on them, and don't fall into the trap of considering them a priority. Once you finish everything else on your plate, you can then evaluate how much time you want to devote to polishing something.

If the task is at 90 percent of the quality you need it to be, it's time to look around at what else needs your attention to bring it from 0 percent to 90 percent. In other words, it's far more helpful to have three tasks completed at 80 percent quality versus one task at 100 percent quality.

When you consciously avoid the items on your don't-do list, you keep yourself focused and streamlined. A don't-do list enables you to know exactly where your path should lead, and what action to take on first. When you're at a fork in the road and each fork looks equally appealing, you're going to be stuck in analysis paralysis (a perpetual debate between options that leaves you motionless in reality). Eliminate some of those forks right off the bat.

Accept the Uncertainty of Action

Part of the reason we overthink is because we want to be *thorough*. If we're not thorough, we feel that we will overlook something to disastrous results. We keep imagining that we must be more prepared to minimize our chances of disastrous failure. We want complete certainty before we expose ourselves to risk, and thus, we never get off our couch.

But there's no possible way for us to control everything in our world. Trying to do so is usually a surefire recipe for chaos, inefficiency, and massive disappointment. Because of it, we therefore have to allow the reality that we'll always have a certain degree of uncertainty in our lives. That's where we must start with this point. Any time you take action, you open yourself up to uncertainty, and this scares us.

Cognitive therapist Dr. Robert Leahy explains why there is such dread over looming uncertainty: "People worry because they think something bad will happen or could happen, so they activate a hyper-vigilant strategy of worry and think that 'If I worry, I can prevent this bad thing from happening or catch it early.'"

We believe that uncertainty, or rather, the lack of certainty, will lead to a bad outcome. We still feel this way if the uncertainty ends up creating a negligible or even positive effect after the fact. Therefore, we hold predictability as the highest standard and volatile unpredictability as the lowest. *Uncertainty equals disaster.*

Inaction feels 100 percent predictable and therefore safe. That's nowhere close to the truth; nevertheless, we spin our wheels and construct crude fortresses against the unpredictable. A healthier mindset doesn't just leave room for uncertainty—it *embraces* it. If you want complete assurance in the success of your actions, you're just waiting for something that has never been possible and is never going to show itself to you. You must come to terms with a low degree of discomfort through uncertainty in your life.

After all, how much uncertainty do you already allow in your life as a regular occurrence? Every time you get in a vehicle, you're subjecting yourself to the unknown. Any time you change cities, shift jobs, or take a vacation, you're taking a number of risks. But they're not standing in the way of your work or leisure. Why are they any different? All you can control is your actions, and outcomes are a completely separate matter.

Uncertainty is inherent in any action, even if you've done it a thousand times before. You just feel more confident about it, so you ignore the uncertainty.

You have no choice but to live with this uncertainty—so acceptance of it is just a step above that. Accept the reality, digest it, and allow that there's no immediate resolution—then continue doing what you need to do. Knock out the required work like you normally would. Make rational and level-headed plans to find a new career if you have to. Develop your networks and friends for life away from the center of action. It's not easy to be uncertain, but there are simple ways to endure it and not let it overtake you.

I know what you're thinking: "If we accept uncertainty and merrily embrace it, then what happens when we really *do* get a terrible outcome? Won't this cause us to underestimate how awful the uncertain thing really is? What if acceptance of whatever's out there causes us to disregard warning signs or cautions, and the whole thing becomes a catastrophe because we 'accepted uncertainty'? And then won't we be haunted by remorse for the rest of our lives because we didn't do enough?"

That's understandable. But I didn't say to *ignore* the possibility of uncertain, adverse events. Accepting uncertainty isn't the same thing as dismissing it as irrelevant.

What we're talking about is *reasonable* uncertainty. That means both a reasonable *amount* of uncertainty and what uncertainty could reasonably *happen*. For example, if you're opening a new shop on a busy street, there are a few things you could be reasonably worried about—given that you don't let such worries cripple your efforts.

Getting absolute certainty is impossible—it will never happen. You'll just continue to seek it and never move ahead as a result. And some things will always be outside of your control no matter how much you worry about them. Any type of action or movement you strive to take will carry uncertainty with it. It's unavoidable, but also freeing because it changes your expectations.

Takeaways and action steps:

- Overthinking is exactly what you want to avoid in your quest to take action. You truly cannot think and do at the same time, so no matter how productive your mental machinations feel, just know that 99.99 percent of the time, they are holding you back from what you should be doing.

- Overthinking is when your brain is too active with too much information. This is when you should employ the Ostrich Theory and willful ignorance to your benefit. Ostriches, of course, have been mythologized to bury their heads in the sand to avoid danger. Likewise, humans similarly ignore information to avoid danger. Use this to your advantage for once and practice restricting your flow of information and inquiries to become willfully ignorant so you can focus on action rather than thinking.

    - Action step: Limit the amount of information you take in. However many sources you typically consult, cut them in half. Put a cap on your research and rumination time. Practice willful ignorance and realize that not everything is important or urgent. Try to ignore negative indicators based on immediacy, source, category, or diminishing returns.

- A premortem analysis is when you analyze the potential causes of failure before you take action. How is this helpful? Because it makes you focus on one of the few important factors in action—failure—instead of spinning your wheels over other irrelevant aspects.

    o Action step: Perform a premortem analysis! But make sure that you don't just add this train of thought to your mental to-do list; it should *replace* the other topics you think about. Work backwards from your normal train of thought: ask yourself how potential failures will occur, what the likely causes are, and what solutions you can implement. Chances are most of your mental chatter is not focused in this most important direction.

- A don't-do list is predicated on the fact that most of us know what we should be doing—we are usually just avoiding it or procrastinating. However, most of us get stuck in overthinking because we don't know what we *shouldn't* be doing. This list takes care of that and articulates three types of tasks for you to avoid. You may find that after eliminating these distractions, you'll be left with a clear path for what to take action on.

  - Action step: Create your don't-do list. Make it as long and detailed as possible with the tasks that have diminishing returns, are waiting on other people, and don't add value to your goals. Have the intention of knowing exactly what to focus on after you're done.

- One of the biggest reasons we overthink? Uncertainty in the outcome, which is related to insecurity and fear. We want to be thorough to the point that we know we will not fail if we act. Unfortunately, that's impossible, and if you attempt it you're just going to stay on the sidelines, searching for something that doesn't exist. Uncertainty to most of us is nearly synonymous with negativity, but that's not the reality. Uncertainty is omnipresent in everything we do, and it is actually freeing to change your expectations. Once you accept uncertainty, you'll be willing to risk a little more and take to action a bit quicker.

- o Action step: Think about the ways you already accept uncertainty in your life. In fact, compose a short list and rate the relative probabilities and levels of danger. You could be hit with a car every time you cross the road. Eventually, when you accept that fact, it just fades into background static. Remember this when you are faced with something potentially nerve-wracking or fearful.

Chapter 2. Err on the Side of Action

The best way to predict the future is to create it. - Unknown

One of the (many) problems with a lifetime of not taking action is that your first instinct will be to freeze. You may feel that it's safer to maintain the status quo instead of making a move, or you may just feel uncomfortable acting without analyzing things to death. Whatever the case, you have found yourself unconsciously erring on the side of inaction.

You may have heard of what's known as the *fight or flight response*. This is when we interpret a stimulus in the world to be dangerous, which ratchets up our adrenaline and alertness and readies our bodies to either flee at full speed or engage in a fight to the death. What's less frequently mentioned is that this response actually has a third component—*freezing*. For most, this is when the adrenaline rush is so extreme that we are essentially left frozen in shock. For those who have made a habit of avoiding action, this is our default response no matter what happens.

It's easier said than done to break these patterns, but this chapter contains a few ways to err on the side of action and get moving more frequently and consistently.

Get a Little Uncomfortable

The action you want rarely happens when you're in your comfort zone. In fact, that's probably true with anything you want. It's not going to come easy, and you will have to endure something uncomfortable, new, and difficult to achieve it.

If you are too comfortable with your current job, you won't feel the need to push your boundaries to seek a promotion or pay raise. You won't learn new skills or strive for something better. You figure that good enough is good enough, and so inaction will be your way of living. We call this sort of sloth *comfortable inaction*. Things may not be ideal, but you're comfortable enough (or not uncomfortable enough), and thus no action will be taken.

You can think of it as your tolerance for discomfort being higher than average. It's knowing that you're slowly gaining weight, but not changing your eating habits because you can still squeeze into your favorite pair of jeans. Or, for instance, it's understanding that your business's monthly revenues have been decreasing by 5 percent for five months, but not changing your business model because you're still paying your bills without a problem.

Comfortable inaction can also rear its head in small everyday occurrences like lying in bed, being slightly cold, but not wanting to get out of bed to close your windows. You'd be warmer and more comfortable if you took action, but without it, you feel adequate and like you would be able to fall asleep regardless.

Whatever your short-term needs and desires, they are being adequately met, so there is no reason to change your life around. Initially, comfortable inaction may seem completely harmless. After all, you've already found ways to live with the problem or to mentally deal, right? You rationalize to yourself that if something urgent happened, you would be able to spring into action. (But who's to say that you wouldn't simply increase your threshold for discomfort and wave off most problems as issues you can just cope with?)

What makes comfortable inaction so damaging? Because everything compounds and grows over time, and if you're not careful, you will unknowingly end up in a situation that is untenable and far past any boundaries you may have set for yourself. This is best exemplified with a frog trapped in a pot of water that is slowly coming to a boil. If the frog was suddenly thrown in a pot of boiling water, he would jump out, but if he is in the water as it gradually grows hotter, then he doesn't perceive the growing danger and boils to death out of a lack of self-awareness.

There may be urgent emergencies down the line, but for the time being, you're more comfortable doing nothing. Understand that even if you may be comfortable right now, it doesn't mean you will be so forever. Constantly settling is not how you get what you want in life. Stop setting aside things for later when you can handle them right now.

Generally speaking, successful people have a bias for action. Their default mode is to spot issues and then execute as fast as possible, because they know that's the only way to get what they want in this world. They don't get sidetracked by distraction, fears, or even comfort. Perhaps they have even conditioned themselves to be uncomfortable with inaction, an enviable mental space to occupy.

The human mind is great at coming up with excuses for not taking a risk. After all, why would you want to change anything if you're already in an acceptable situation? This is the million-dollar question: how can you use this knowledge of comfortable inaction to avoid falling into its trap?

Picture that you are living in a house in Hawaii close to a volcano. In one scenario, you turn on the news radio to hear that researchers have estimated that the volcano near you will be active within the next one hundred years. You figure you won't be around to care, so inaction it is for you. In another scenario, you turn on the news radio and discover that researchers have estimated the volcano to be active within the following two months. You start packing up your belongings in cardboard boxes immediately.

What was the difference? Inaction was no longer comfortable; in fact, it was painful. Thus, to break out of comfortable inaction, you must make inaction as uncomfortable as possible. Imagine all the long-term and short-term consequences of inaction with as much detail as you can. Project into the future and visualize all the eventualities. In fact, let your imagination run wild as you picture the potential failure, rejection, and how far behind you will be. This helps in two main ways: First, it snaps you to awareness of what's at stake in your life beyond your current sense of laziness. Second, amplifying pains and discomforts creates a sense of urgency that will push you to act to stop that pain.

Suppose you've been dreaming about leaving your desk job and building something of your own, but you never actually do it because you are comfortable with receiving a fixed amount on a fixed date to pay your bills. That seems like a pretty reasonable excuse to stay in your zone of inaction, right?

But think about all the opportunities you are missing, as well as the ways you are stifling your growth by staying. Amplify the positives from action and negatives from inaction.

Positives from action: You could be earning more money, or you could be working for only four hours a week instead of forty. You could be going on a nice vacation every month or, even better, working from exotic locales. You could be proud of building something from the ground up. You could retire early. You could laugh at all your naysayers. You could be your own boss instead of a perpetual cog in the machine. You have always dreamed of working for yourself. Your worst-case scenario is to end up exactly where you are right now.

Negatives from inaction: You are miserable at your job. You hate your supervisors. You have a long commute. You will never advance further than you already have. You don't feel passionately about your work. Competition increases every day. Both your opportunity and ambition will decrease with age. You are never going to build a business if not now.

Is it really that scary to take a risk on something you've never tried before? When you think about it hard enough, you might realize that inaction is actually a lot scarier. Inaction amounts to a lot of wasted time, but taking action makes wasted time impossible.

Tiny Steps

Very few people want to go to work when it's raining cats and dogs outside. It's an enormous burden to overcome mentally. You'll get soaked, your shoes and socks will be puddles, and you'll freeze from head to toe. Oh, and your only umbrella is broken. It's such a burden that you don't even want to go through the motions of getting dressed and putting on your boots. You feel defeated before you even begin.

Sometimes a horrendously rainy day can feel just like trying to take action and get started.

When we're faced with huge tasks that feel insurmountable, it's like looking through a window out at the rain. It's such an obstacle that everything feels impossible and pointless. We drag our feet, discourage ourselves, and bitterly complain the whole time. Most of us will probably just stay inside the entire day with a cup of hot chocolate and never get our day started.

Similarly, a single huge task, such as "finish the two-hundred-page report," can certainly sound imposing, if not impossible. It's just so discouraging to start something like that because you feel that it will never end and you will never make any progress. To some extent, that's true, because even writing ten pages is only completing 5 percent of the task. Imagine how hopeless you would feel.

However, what if you were to break that monumental project up into tiny, easy, individual tasks you could get to work on immediately, as well as see instant progress? For example: preparing the template, finding the first three sources, creating a bibliography, outlining five hundred words of the first section, and so on. Actually, it can go much smaller yet: choosing the fonts, writing the chapter titles, organizing the desk, formatting the document, turning the computer on, sitting down for five minutes, or writing just one sentence.

The smaller, the better. Otherwise, you're starting each day staring at the equivalent of a torrential downpour. When you break up your tasks into as tiny pieces as possible, you are creating ways to keep your brain happy and motivated for action. Anything difficult is only a series of easy things.

One of the biggest hurdles to taking action is looking at tasks as huge, inseparable boulders. It's intimidating and discouraging, and when those emotions arise, it's easy to avoid action because tackling a boulder is a tough sell. Unfortunately, this is a habit that plagues most people. They see only massive boulders and allow themselves to get emotionally thrown off track.

Break up your big tasks into smaller activities and keep repeating until the tasks you have before you are so easy, you can do them within a few minutes. Create small, manageable chunks that will be psychologically uplifting and acceptable, and you'll increase your action instantly. Make your to-do list as long and articulated as possible, with as many small tasks as you can list. Instead of boulders, think in terms of pebbles—a pebble is something you can handle instantly, without any effort and even with little thought. In fact, make each task so small it's almost like you're not doing anything at all.

Can you start a fire only with big logs? You might be able to, but it would be difficult. It's much easier to start with kindling, paper scraps, and small pieces of wood that burn easily. Small steps can take you to the top of the hill and let you roll down the other side to seize momentum. They help you break the inertia that leads to passivity.

Let's take an example that we're all familiar with: working out. You want to lose one hundred pounds, a hefty goal. If you go into the gym every day thinking that you want to lose one hundred pounds, you're going to fail. It's a huge, enormous boulder of a goal. It might sound grand to proclaim, but in reality, it is going to be very hard to stick to because of how unbelievable it sounds.

You won't see much progress on a daily or even weekly basis, and you will understandably become discouraged. It's too much to face at once, like the rainy day from the beginning of the chapter. So what if you approach your weight loss target by breaking it into small, manageable increments (goals) and tasks?

This might look something like setting a reasonable weekly weight loss goal, creating daily objectives of eating specific foods (and not eating others), and drinking water every hour. Eat one hundred fewer calories per meal. Go on walks after each meal. Drink only half your soda. Eat five fewer fries each meal. Cook once a week. Buy the low-calorie version of snacks. Substitute water for fruit juice. Now those sound much more palatable and achievable—easy, even.

If you hit your weekly weight loss goal and successfully drink water every hour, it is far easier to stay motivated and focused. Meeting your smaller weekly target will give you a sense of accomplishment, whereas making an insignificant dent in your total goal (one hundred pounds) will only leave you feeling discouraged and as if the task ahead is too great to achieve.

These are small tasks that, if done consistently and correctly, will lead to your overall goal of losing one hundred pounds. These tiny steps and frequent victories will encourage and motivate you to take action.

Depending on our mood, even saying "I'm going to write two hundred words" can feel like a twenty-mile march to the sea. In this case, it's not even a tiny step—it's a portion of a step—that we struggle with. One way to get the ball rolling no matter how you feel is to change your phrasing. "I'm going to finish that" turns into "I'm going to get started on that." The point of this, just like with tiny steps, is to make your threshold for starting as low as possible. In fact, you want to make it so low that it's nearly indistinguishable from the laziness of not acting at all.

The 40-70 Rule

Former US Secretary of State Colin Powell has a rule of thumb about coming to a point of action. He says that any time you face a hard choice, you should have *no less* than 40 percent and *no more* than 70 percent of the information you need to make that decision. In that range, you have enough knowledge to make an informed choice, but not so much intelligence that you lose your resolve and inject hesitation and paralysis into your considerations.

If you have less than 40 percent of the information you need, you're essentially shooting from the hip. You don't know quite enough to move forward and will probably make a lot of mistakes. Conversely, if you chase down more data until you get more than 70 percent of what you need (and it's unlikely that you'll truly need anything above this level), you could get overwhelmed and become uncertain. The opportunity may have passed you by, and someone else may have beaten you by starting already.

This is the zone of inaction—you want 100 percent information, and although it's never possible, it's a zone of safety. Safety from uncertainty, insecurity, and all the rest.

But in that sweet spot between 40 and 70 percent, you have enough to go on and can let your intuition guide your decisions. In the context of Colin Powell, this is where effective leaders are made: the people whose instincts point in the right direction are the ones who will lead their organization to success. This is also where you should battle procrastination before it becomes too late. You should feel a certain amount of uncertainty, or even lack of confidence—it's natural, and anything else is an unrealistic expectation. More often than not, what you are searching for will only be gained through *beginning*. As mentioned, the first step will be your most valuable tool in learning and preparation, rather than hours of planning.

We can replace the word "information" with other motivators: 40–70 percent of experience, 40–70 percent reading or learning, 40–70 percent confidence, or 40–70 percent planning. While we're taking action, we learn, gain confidence, and gain momentum.

When you try to achieve more than 70 percent information (or confidence, experience, etc.), your lack of speed can destroy your momentum or stem your interest, effectively meaning nothing's going to happen. There is a high likelihood of gaining nothing further from surpassing this threshold.

For example, let's say you're opening up a cocktail bar, which involves buying a lot of different types of liquor. You're going to wait until you're 100 percent ready with your liquor before opening. Yet you can't expect to have absolutely all the liquor you will ever need when the doors are ready to open. It's impossible to be able to serve any drink a customer orders.

So, applying this rule, you'd wait until you had at least 40 percent of your available inventory prepared. This would establish momentum. Then, if you could get more than half of what you need, you'd be in pretty good shape to open. You might not be able to make absolutely every drink in the bartenders' guide, but you'll have enough on-hand to cover the staple drinks with a couple variations. If you have around 50–60 percent inventory, you're more than ready.

When the remaining inventory arrives, you'll already be in action and can just incorporate that new inventory into your offerings. If you waited until you had 70 percent or more inventory to open, you could find yourself stuck in neutral for longer than you wanted to be. Imagine what would happen if you waited until you had 100 percent of what you needed—rare vintages of wines and exotic vodkas from across the world. You'd never open.

So let's simplify: If you want to arrange a date, you only need three elements: who, when, and where. If you need to find a hospital, you only need to know the specialist you want to see, the cost, and the location. If you want to start a business, you only need to think about what you can do tomorrow to move toward your goal, not necessarily what your ideal business is.

You'll end up with more action than not. Waiting until you have 40 percent of what you need to make a move isn't a way of staying inside your comfort zone—you're actively planning what you need to do to get out, which is just fine (as long as it's not over-planning). For all intents and purposes, the minimum effective dose of information or preparation you need is far lower than you imagine it to be.

Beat Indecision

Action has many enemies. Excessive planning, perfectionism, fear, laziness—just to name a few. It's a shame because each of those enemies, despite whatever protective instinct they fulfill, only serves one purpose: to keep you still.

An underestimated enemy of action is *indecision*. Unlike other parts of inaction that are plagued by laziness or plain avoidance, you may actually have a good intent with indecision. You want to take action, but the problem is that you are incapable of choosing from what's in front of you. In part, the don't-do list and premortem analysis can help you with indecision, but here are some specific ways to make decisions quicker than you ever thought possible.

The first point on defeating indecision is to realize that almost every choice is reversible to some degree. Almost nothing is forever and immediately harmful; there is usually some sort of grace period when nothing is permanent if you don't wish it to be. Therefore, it makes sense to dip your toe into one option to see what happens and gain some information instead of standing at the fork in the road until you starve to death. Make a decision with the full intent of backtracking—you'll feel better making it because you see an easy route out, but you've just broken your inertia.

You learn so much more by taking an option, even for a bit, than from hemming and hawing at the crossroads. Only in the process will you learn more about it and how it feels. In essence, commit to an option and follow it for a while, because it's probably reversible, and you learn more from committing and following through.

If you are trying to decide between moving to New York or Texas, are you going to gain more information by visiting neither and continuing to debate with yourself, or by visiting one, seeing how you feel about it, and going through some motions to gain information? You'd visit Texas and start looking into rental prices, how to attain your driver's license, the local job economy, and the prevalence of healthy food. Make a small commitment, follow the path, and then re-evaluate again. The important part is getting away from complete stillness.

Second, apply strict boundaries to help you make the choice for you. This streamlines your process and reduces the amount of thinking you have to do. For example, if you are struggling with what restaurant to pick for dinner, you might apply filters of healthy, inexpensive, within a ten-minute drive, and not hamburgers. After you set these parameters, you might only have one or two choices left over. It's like when you shop online and apply filters for size, style, price, and color; suddenly, you're left with only two shirts to buy.

If you're left with zero choices, remove one or two filters and work backward until you can make an easy yet satisfactory decision. You'll be left with options that are within your criteria, and at that point, what does it really matter? You can choose at random at this point with no loss in happiness or effectiveness, as you've successfully ignored everything that you *don't* care about.

A corollary to setting boundaries is to first identify a *default choice* if you can't decide within a set amount of time. Pick your default upfront and then set a time limit where if you can't choose something else, you automatically go with the default. For instance, with your significant other, your default restaurant is an Italian joint. If you can't choose a different restaurant within five minutes, then to Italy you go. This saves time, but the act of creating the default is important because you will have automatically selected something that fits your requirements or desires. You'll be happy in either case, in other words.

In many instances, the default is what you had in mind the entire time and where you were probably going to end up regardless of the endless debate. You go through the mental exercise of choosing a "default" with the idea that you accept ending up there even if you considered other choices.

For the third aspect of conquering indecisiveness, realize that you might have a drive to make the "perfect" decision with absolutely no downsides, no opportunity costs, and no second thoughts. Well, that's tough to do on a daily basis. Instead of seeking perfection, seek satisfaction of your needs—that's what really matters for 99 percent of our decisions.

If something checks all your boxes, that's all you need to beat your indecision. When you aim for perfection, you tend to start running up against the law of diminishing returns, which states that the amount of effort you put into something is no longer worth the return you gain. Oh, and a perfect decision is also usually impossible or nonexistent.

For example, you might spend one hundred dollars on a pair of nice shoes. At that price point, they will be well constructed, sturdy, and fashionable. What if you were to spend two thousand dollars on a similar pair of shoes? They'd still be well constructed, sturdy, and fashionable. So in most instances, consider the primary goal of your action—shoes take you from Point A to Point B and should contain a modicum of style.

This begs the question, were the pricier shoes worth the extra money over the cheaper pair? For most people, no. There is a law of diminishing returns where the more expensive shoes don't make a difference in any relevant way. How nice can a pair of shoes get? Unless the more expensive shoes are self-cleaning with automatic lacing, you are spending more for essentially the same return.

You probably aren't shooting for life-changing restaurants every night of the week. In this case, your compulsion to make a perfect choice is wasted energy. Eating is the goal, not choosing a perfect meal. Unless you are making life-impacting choices that you will feel the repercussions of for years, attempting to make a perfect choice is silly. The difference between the "perfect" choice and the "good enough" choice will be negligible, and you might not even feel it, or remember it the next day. There won't be consequences that make a difference in the long term, so what is the sense in spending additional time on it?

In fact, aim for adequate, or even imperfect and flawed. Suddenly, you'll see that it's far easier to make a decision if you lighten up the standards that you've probably arbitrarily placed on yourself.

A famous comedian has clever input on this matter: "My rule is that if you have someone or something that gets seventy percent approval, you just do it, 'cause here's what happens. The fact that other options go away immediately brings your choice to eighty, because the pain of deciding is over." This is surprisingly similar to what former Secretary of State Colin Powell has to say on the matter.

Fourth, to make better and quicker decisions, engage in intentionally judgmental thinking. This is the type of thinking you have probably tried to repress, but it will be very beneficial for your decision-making. Think in black-and-white terms and reduce your decisions down to one to three main points. Overgeneralize and don't look at the subtleties of your options. Willfully ignore the gray area and don't rationalize or justify statements by saying "But . . ." or "That's not *always* true . . ."

Focus on what really moves the needle for you and ignore things that, while they matter, aren't the most important. Sometimes, consuming less information will help this process because you are focused on a smaller set of factors. Let's go back to the example of choosing a restaurant for dinner. How can you think more in black-and-white terms about something like this? Simply reduce your restaurant choices down to what you might categorize as a first impression. Restaurant A is a place for burgers, despite the fact that there are five menu items that are not burgers. It doesn't matter—in black-and-white terms, it's a burger place.

Restaurant B is expensive, despite the fact that it has five cheaper items. It doesn't matter—in black-and-white terms, it's expensive. Restaurant C is far away, even though if you hit good traffic, it's not too far. It doesn't matter—in black-and-white terms, it is far.

Seeing options in black and white basically generalizes their traits and removes their subtleties. Remember, if we're talking about destroying indecision, this is one of the best things you can do. If you have a hazy stereotype of your two options and the stakes are relatively low, then that's all the information you need.

A final method to be intentionally judgmental is to sum up your options in one short sentence only, no commas or addendums allowed. You aren't allowed to elaborate on anything. When you try this, you'll notice you can only end up with broad strokes, such as "It's a burger place that's ten minutes away" versus "Well, they serve burgers, but they also have lasagna and tacos. It's ten minutes away, but I think we can get there faster." Which one is going to be easier for you to ignore or accept? Remember, the idea is faster action, and not necessarily trying to optimize every decision that you come across.

Making quick decisions is certainly a major pillar in erring on the side of action. Consider that indecision is another name for overthinking, and remember, we can't *think* and *do* at the same time. For the purposes of this book, motion is always preferred to analysis (beyond a certain extent).

Limit Consumption for More Production

It happens all the time. You're sitting down, trying to get in some reading, and by the time you look up, hours have passed. Losing track of time in this pursuit is great if you're being productive, but reading is only productive when it adds actual value to our lives. More often than not, it doesn't!

Consuming information is almost always seen as a net positive. It's what we believe underlies being educated and intelligent, and reading in particular is seen as superior to more passive forms of media consumption.

The point is that it's easy to feel like we're being productive by reading, when all we're actually doing is wasting time in a slightly more intellectual way than binge-watching *Game of Thrones*. When we justify our information consumption in this way, what we're really doing is justifying our procrastination. We use information as a procrastination tool. Reclaim your lost time and get started by going on an *information diet*.

Information diets aren't about being less educated or cutting out leisure reading; they're simply about considering our end goals and if we are unconsciously doing something detrimental to those goals. Too often and too easily, we get *sucked into* information, and when we consume, we cannot produce.

But how do we decide what information is worth consuming, and what's worth leaving on the shelf? How do we even know what information is sucking up our time? Begin by taking an honest look at how you spend your time. You can do this in the following steps.

1. Survey your information consumption.
2. Remove at least 50 percent of the least valuable content you consume and cut the noise from your information diet.
3. View descriptions of information pieces as pitches for your time and attention.
4. Say no more often.

5. Consider cutting entire information forms from your life.
6. Monitor how much of any one information source you're consuming.

For one week, make a list of every type of media you consume, from your Facebook feed to *War and Peace*.

It's important to know exactly where your time is going so you can make cuts. You might be surprised to find you're scrolling through social media feeds for hours per day, or you may discover that you spend far too many hours inhaling the latest bestseller. It doesn't matter what you're consuming when you begin this process; what matters is that you identify where your time is going so that you can redirect it toward activities that need to get done.

After you make your list, you'll see a lot of different mediums. Social media, books, magazines, television, podcasts, and similar items will probably populate your list. Some are genuinely valuable; they help you be more creative, bring you joy, and make you and your life better. They assist you in your work, or they are flat-out required research to keep you progressing and growing. This doesn't all have to be edifying; genuinely enjoying a TV show or other product can be a good enough reason to keep it in your life.

But right off the bat, you can also see that some of these are useless and keep you stuck in inaction. You'll find a lot of items that you didn't actively choose to watch or read; they were just there, in front of you, and you consumed them on autopilot. Autopilot as unconscious consumption is the real enemy here.

You can tell something should be cut out of your life when it has no current or practical utility. Only information we can immediately apply to our current situation is important. This is what happens when we fall into the Wikipedia rabbit hole, for instance—suddenly we end up learning about 17th-century woodworking when we were only trying to become knowledgeable about one historical figure.

Hypothetical or *just in case* information can also be useful, but most of the time it shouldn't be your current focus. This is like researching the type of clothing you should buy when you lose 50 pounds—it's a legitimate concern, but not at the present moment.

Plenty of other information you take in will be downright useless—you neither enjoy it nor find facts within it that can be applied to better your life. It was just placed in front of you, and you consumed it without realizing it. These are cereal boxes, advertisements, and vapid entertainment news that are just entertaining enough to suck us in but are mostly without substance.

Once you cut out 50 percent of the least useful media you consume, you'll have that much more spare time to devote to the things you've been putting off. That's way better than wasting time skimming through posts or blankly watching a show you don't care about. This tactic in itself isn't a cure for procrastination, but it does help when you are at the fork in the road, and if a distraction is less handy, it's one less obstacle to working.

It helps to view television, books, articles, and podcasts as pitches for your time and attention. Both are finite; everything we consume also consumes our time and energy. In addition, we can't produce at the same time as we're consuming. It's impossible to do both at once.

At this point, it should be obvious that being entertained or educated doesn't come free of cost, even when no money is being charged. Even when items are free, they're not without cost to your work and productivity.

Given all of this, it makes sense to be discriminating about what we spend our time consuming and to be especially careful before we let something new catch our eye. Before watching or reading anything, even something you know you'll like, read or listen to a short description and consider whether the object is worth your time. You can even do this with works you already know by consciously reminding yourself what you're going to find before loading up a website or sitting down for a film. The important thing here is consciousness. When we think about the cost of frittering away time on subpar entertainment, we're less likely to indulge—or to waste time.

In addition to considering the inherent cost of consuming information, there's a much simpler way to change our habits: commit to saying no. Merely deciding to stop indulging in media a set number of times, say three times per week, can radically change how we interact with the world.

Without consciously setting limits, it's easy to see keeping up with friends on social media as an obligation or to feel like we have to finish watching the show we like, but none of that's compulsory. At all points, we control our action. We can always say no.

While filtering things out of your life and preventing your newfound autonomy from being snatched from you, consider the mediums that deliver low-value information to you. Often, we find ourselves drifting back to the same time sinks over and over again. When we notice these patterns, it's worth considering excising the whole medium from our lives. Whether it's getting rid of cable TV, committing to a life without social media, or deciding to spend less time reading books, making a decisive change can prevent the need to say no over and over again.

Finally, consider how much time you're sinking into all the remaining forms of media you consume. How much time is spent on television, reading, listening to podcasts, or scrolling through feeds? If you spend too long in any one place, it's likely you're devoting time to those activities because they're automatic, not because you're really enjoying them. Cutting back in those areas can leave more time for the good things in life.

Learning to make cutbacks on attention expenditures lets us focus on information that helps us grow, learn, and thrive. Fortunately, the process of reducing the noise from your media streams can be approached in many ways, allowing anyone to make small—or even major—changes in their routines.

Once we've established a newer, more conscious routine, it'll be that much easier to find time for the people and things we truly love and to finish tasks we'd otherwise be inclined to set aside. That sure beats being constantly stressed about the work we're avoiding.

Takeaways and action steps:

- What does it mean to err on the side of action? Simply, it means that instead of freezing or analyzing, you should attempt to make your default response action. Have an action bias.
- The first way to err on the side of action is to break through what's known as comfortable inaction. This is where you feel that things are good enough, so you might as well not disrupt the status quo.

This is where we get sayings like "good is the enemy of great" and so on, but it's true—you will never live the way you want if you are too comfortable where you are now.

- o Action step: You aren't uncomfortable enough to take action, so increase the amount of discomfort that comes along with inaction so you have no choice but to act. For something you are trying to break past a plateau on, allow your imagination to run wild on the various negative consequences you will face. Think about the rewards you will miss. Think about the short and long-term repercussions. Once these seem more urgent and tangible, action will be far easier.

- It's tough to get started when you're facing something huge. You already dread it because you know it will not feel rewarding and you won't be able to finish anytime soon. That in itself is discouraging. Therefore, break up your tasks into as tiny steps as possible, steps

so small that it's almost no different from your status quo of inaction.
- Action step: Break down a task you've been dreading into ten small, individual steps. Can you break it down into fifteen, and then twenty? How does it feel to achieve something, no matter how small? I bet it feels great.

- The 40-70 Rule popularized by Colin Powell states that you should get started with no less than 40 percent of the information you feel is necessary, but no more than 70 percent. For our purposes, focus on getting started with 40 percent—what might feel like an insufficient amount of information. But in reality, you've already hit the point of diminishing returns, and anything else will be learned more effectively along the way.
  - Action step: Apply the 40-70 Rule to elements other than information: confidence, planning, learning, and preparing. Write down the top ten details you need to complete something. Now try

eliminating three of those details. Did it make a difference? For that matter, how many of the ten do you actually need to get started? To simply begin, you likely need nowhere close to ten.

- Indecision is basically overthinking by another name, and it is an equivalent obstacle to erring on the side of action and gaining momentum. Indecision is defeatable in many ways, with the common thread between many of the methods being some sort of pickiness.
    - Action step: Attempt to apply all the tactics described to something you are having trouble deciding on. These include: commit with the intent of backtracking, apply strict boundaries, utilize a default choice, seek satisfactory choices over perfect ones, engage in intentionally judgmental thinking, and be purposefully general and vague. Which one works best for you and helps you reach a decision the quickest?

- Finally, you can limit your information consumption. Very little of what we consume is helpful or even relevant. Most of it is also consumed unconsciously, without us realizing that we are spending so much time and effort on it—we get sucked in. Cultivate self-awareness, curate your consumption and reduce your media sources so you can devote your limited energy toward work and motion.
    - Action step: make a list of what you consume for a week, and make a resolution to cut down on at least 50 percent of it. Preview information before you engage with it, and view everything as a pitch for your time and energy.

Chapter 3. The Take-Action Mindset

Take the first step in faith. You don't have to see the whole staircase, just take the first step. - Dr. Martin Luther King Jr.

We've talked about the various ways that you can be galvanized into action. This chapter focuses on the mindsets regarding action—your perspective and overall view about motion versus stillness.

Our actions depend wholly on our thoughts, and no matter how much we incentivize ourselves, if we can't change the way we think about action, we're doomed. For instance, one common concept is the fixed mindset versus the growth mindset.

The *fixed* mindset says that intelligence, talent, ability, and performance are all firmly determined from cradle to grave—they can't change or grow. You are what you are, and if you don't have something by now, you'll never have it.

This leads to a whole lot of roadblocks in the process itself, because what's the purpose in trying if you don't think you have it in you?

The *growth* mindset is fundamentally different because it assumes change and growth are possible. Whatever and wherever you are right now is just a starting place from which to develop and improve. In this approach, nothing is impossible because it takes the position that learning and growth are always rewarded in some way.

You can imagine how possessing either of these mindsets can drastically change your life. Remember, thoughts belie actions.

Motivation Follows Action

The first way to impart a take-action mindset is to understand the real way in which motivation appears.

It would be five million times easier to achieve our goals if we all knew how to motivate ourselves 100 percent of the time. It would be like pressing a magical button that jolts us out of bed and into work. Whenever our energy is faltering, we could just press the button again, and we'd be injected with another dose of that good stuff and become correspondingly productive. The closest legal thing we have to this is coffee, but even that has waning effects.

It's easier to feel motivated when you like a project or when you're doing something you are genuinely passionate about. But let's be realistic—there are days when just the mere act of leaving your bed is a challenge and a huge accomplishment. For most of us, we don't enjoy what we do enough to feel motivated by it. An artist may be inspired to bring her visions into reality, but for the rest of us? We're really just trying to scrape together enough willpower to get us through our days. This is all to clarify motivation's role in taking action and getting started.

Whatever your goals, motivation plays an important role and can spell the difference between success and failure. It's one of the most important ingredients to influence your drive and ambition, but we're thinking about it *all wrong*.

When we think about motivation, we want something that will light a spark in us and make us jump up from the couch and dive deeply into our tasks. We want *motivation that causes action*. There are a few problems with this, namely the fact you're probably looking for something that doesn't exist, and that's going to keep you waiting on the sidelines, out of action, and out of the race. This type of motivation, if you ever find it, is highly unreliable. If you feel you need motivation that causes action, you are doing it wrong.

For instance, a writer who feels they are unable to write without some form of motivation or inspiration is going to stare at a blank page for hours. End of story.

The truth is, you should plan for life *without* a motivating kick start. Seeking that motivation creates a prerequisite and additional barrier to action. Get into the habit of proceeding without it. And surprisingly, this is where you'll find what you were seeking. *Action leads to motivation*, and more motivation, and eventually momentum.

The more you work for something, the more meaningful it becomes to you. Your own actions will be your fuel to move forward. After you've taken your first step and have seen progress from your efforts, motivation will come easier and more naturally, as will inspiration and discipline. You'll fall into a groove, and suddenly, you'll be in your work mood/mode. The first step will always be the hardest, but the second step won't be quite as difficult.

For repetition's sake, forget motivation; get started, and you'll *become* motivated. Taking the first step is tough, but consider that aside from motivation, just getting started gives you many other things.

For instance, confidence also follows action. After all, how do you expect to be confident about something when you haven't even tried? A taste of action tells you that everything will be okay and you have nothing to fear. This is confidence rooted in firsthand experience, which is easier to find than the false confidence you get from trying to convince yourself before the fact that you can succeed.

Public speaking is almost always a scary proposition. Consider how you might try to find confidence that causes action: you would tell yourself it will all be fine, imagine the audience in their underwear, and remind yourself of your hours of rehearsal. Now consider how you might find confidence after getting started—how action can cause confidence. "I did it and it was fine" is an easier argument to make versus "I haven't done it yet, but I think it will be fine."

The most important takeaway here is to not wait until you are 100 percent ready before you take the first step. It will probably never feel like you're completely prepared. But starting down the road will motivate you more than anything else will before the fact, so allow your actions to propel you and build confidence. Change your expectations regarding motivation, and remove the self-imposed requirements you have for yourself.

No More "Zero Days"

Sometimes just thinking about "taking action" might give you a headache. It's true that there are only so many ways to look at the goal of doing more. For a slightly different perspective, consider the mindset of banishing *zero days* from your life. You can combine this with the tiny steps tip from an earlier chapter.

A zero day is a day that you've let slip by without doing anything to achieve your goal, without taking action and doing something tangible outside of pondering. This concept may also apply to a week, an hour, or any other time segment you set (e.g., a zero year is one in which you probably hid out in a cave somewhere and hibernated for 365 days).

Instead of trying to seek action by reaching for a lofty goal, you can take action by trying to avoid a zero day. It's a small shift in mindset that can use your sense of pride and shame to your advantage.

The concept of a zero day simplifies keeping score of how you're doing so far in working toward task completion or the achievement of your dreams. Think of life as a binary: either you're doing something ("1"), or you're not ("0"). Aim for a string of ones instead of zeroes. Make it black and white with no in-between. In other words, see to it that every day, you do something that'll inch you closer to your goal. Don't judge your results other than if you acted or not.

Notice the phrase "inch you closer." The idea of having no more zero days doesn't mean you have to pack every single day with tasks that'll break new ground or catapult you to immediate success. This kind of thinking is what scares most people away from doing anything at all to accomplish their goals. They think they have to exhaust themselves with big, significant tasks every day because they believe simply pecking at something is not worth the effort.

Then, overwhelmed by the idea of having to start on a large task in front of them, they procrastinate and build a string of zeroes instead. Once they accumulate two to three days of zeroes, they then find it easier to let the zeroes persist. They may think, "*Well, I've missed three days at the gym already, so what's the point of ever going at all when I can't be consistent with this?*" So they stop going to the gym. Others may think, "*I have to finish writing an entire chapter today. What's the point of sitting down to write if I'll add only two sentences in there?*" Then, intimidated by the thought of having to complete an entire chapter in one sitting, they procrastinate and end up not writing a single word.

So instead of ranking each day on a scale of one to ten and feeling depressed whenever you fall short, replace the idea of needing a ten to requiring just a one (got something done). It doesn't matter how small a portion of a task you managed to do for the day; it only matters that you at least accomplished something.

Give yourself a one for the day. Strive to rid your calendar of any zero in there, but if you do slip up and get a zero one day, don't feel discouraged. Recover the next day with another one. Once you get into the habit of doing something every single day to move toward your goal, the zeroes in your calendar will diminish until they finally disappear.

For instance, say you need to write a five-chapter research paper over the course of five months. Aim to complete at least one chapter a month, and pledge to have a string of non-zeroes every month. This means that every single day, you need to get something down on paper or do something related to your research paper. Some days, you may feel like an idea machine and jot down a lot of creative ways of looking at your research problem. Other days, you may feel demotivated, but still summarize just a single paragraph of related literature—and that's okay, too. The only thing that matters is that you incur no zero days. It might also help motivate you if you reward yourself at the end of every month that you managed to get through without ever netting a zero.

Another example is setting a "no zero before lunch" policy for yourself. This means that you should accomplish at least a little something toward your goal before every lunch hour. The task you manage to complete may be as simple as scanning the documents needed for your database, or as complex as developing a software system validation procedure. Again, all that matters is that you get something done, whether big or small. It's a way to break the inertia that will cause you to find comfort in inaction.

Keep in mind that you can apply the "no zero" policy to a whole range of time segments, from a span of hours to years. You may choose to commit to a "no-zero hour," a "no-zero day," a "no-zero week," and so on. The important thing is that whatever time segment you set for yourself, you see to it that you do something within it that'll bring you closer to moving toward your goals.

Solution Versus Problem Mindset

This is another divide in thinking that, as you might guess, leads to either thinking or doing.

Problem-oriented thinkers consider the source or cause of the problem rather deeply, whereas solution-oriented thinkers are geared toward coming up with answers for how to fix it. Analyzing the problem is a matter of *thinking*, but searching for a solution to fix it is *doing*.

Someone with the problem-oriented mindset obsesses on the problem itself. They wonder what went wrong. They get upset that it keeps happening. They seek blame and responsibility for the setback, and the only answer they have for the problem is to "avoid it." They are unable to move past their negative feelings regarding a problem or obstacle.

People with the solution-oriented mindset seek answers about a problem and then aggressively looks for ways to fix it. They don't have to remind themselves over and over that the problem is there—they know that. But staying in a feedback loop doesn't help the situation, so the solution-oriented mindset looks for answers that will work now and in the future.

There are times when the problem-oriented approach is appropriate, most commonly if one is trying to find ways to stop the glitch from continually recurring. But unless we take the next step to think about how to solve the obstacles that come up, we're squandering that effort in the big picture.

Solution-oriented thinking takes on a different methodology toward mending a given problem. The first step is to sidestep questions that center on the problem and its causes. Asking *why* takes away from resolution efforts. It's just echoing the problem itself, not coming up with creative and effective solutions. Instead of asking why, the solution-oriented mindset asks, *what now?*

For example, let's say you're having a hard time grasping a certain math concept. You can spend a few minutes wondering why you're having an issue with it. If you go down that rabbit hole, you'll start wondering what the point of learning this particular concept is anyway. Why do you need to know this? What purpose will it serve in your life? With each line of inquiry, you're getting further away from working on the solution—which would entail going back to step one, examining how you arrived at the point you're at now, and looking for alternative routes to get to the answer.

To come up with a solution in this mindset, determine what your existing conditions are now (Point A) and how you eventually want them to turn out (Point B). By gaining a clear understanding of each point and the gap between them, you'll get a much better sense of what you need to do.

Think of the problem in terms of checklists. You could make a list of everything that's going wrong. Alternatively, you could make a list that describes potential solutions. Only one of these checklists is actionable. The only actions you can derive from a list of problems are complaining and fixating on failure. With a list of actions, you have options you can immediately take. Only the action list has real value.

To practice your solution mindset, ask yourself these questions about how to handle a given job or dilemma instead of spinning wheels on the *whys* that don't matter:

- How can I solve this problem?

- How can I address this task?

- How do I get from Point A to Point B?

- What's the first step to solving this problem?

- How do I prepare to get this solution rolling?

Coincidentally, these are all questions that force you into action.

So let's say you're running a cupcake shop. Your product is tasty, but it's not selling well, at least not in comparison to other cupcake shops in the general area. The problem-oriented person would probably grouse about the situation and fixate on the trouble, so much so that they're helpless to improve it. You can check off a big list of factors that are affecting your business—location, no publicity, oversaturation of the market—but once you identify one, you have to start solving it instead of dwelling on it. You have cupcakes to make, damn it.

How can I solve this problem? By proving you have a certain edge over other cupcake makers—better recipes, more savvy publicity, developing something unique that makes you different.

How can I address this task? Let's just take the publicity angle for now. You can make catchier flyers, maybe come up with some funny (or terrible) puns for your cupcakes, look into cheap or free advertising, or have someone stand on the corner in a cupcake costume. (If Subway can do it with people in sandwich costumes, cupcake costumes can't look any more ridiculous.)

How do I get from Point A to Point B? Point A is where you are now—middling success at best. Point B is where you want to be—basically a cupcake magnate. You get from Point A to Point B by making a high-quality, well-marketed product that people go out of their way to obtain.

What's the first step to solving this problem? Sticking with the publicity angle: you look at sample advertising and marketing efforts, preferably from other, successful cupcake companies, and make note of their strategies. Then you try to adapt them to your own style so you won't be copying them and you'll look unique.

How do I prepare to get this solution rolling? Block off some time when you can research and take notes on your publicity research, think of a company, associate, or friend who would be willing to work on it (if you can't do it yourself), and find information on ad styles and rates in local alt-weeklies. Also, find where to incorporate these assets on your website. (You must have a website, right?)

I'm all in favor of quality thinking, analysis, and mental preparation for absolutely everything—but only as much as you need to start *working*. Orient yourself on the problem itself only to the extent that it helps you create a solution. With an action mindset taking precedence over a thinking one, you open up a virtual treasure chest of possibilities that can't come from theorizing alone.

Intentions Versus Actions

"It was not my intention to hurt you..."
"I didn't mean to cause harm..."
"I was trying to make things better..."
"I thought I was doing the right thing..."

How many times have you heard these phrases? Have you actually used them yourself?

Having good intentions is important, but clearly, wanting to do something and *actually* doing something are two very different things. You might genuinely want to do something good, but if you don't follow it up with actions, your intentions mean nothing. We need to clearly distinguish between our intentions and actions, because often, we blur them together and mistake the first for the second. And when we do that, we are fooled into inaction and stillness.

For instance:

- Actions measure your integrity. Intentions don't.
- Actions measure your commitment. Intentions don't.
- Actions measure your impact. Intentions don't.

It's like a husband taking credit and feeling good about the thought of buying flowers for his wife, even though he remained on his couch all night long. Even the smallest deeds have a greater impact than the noblest of intentions, because the world runs only on tangible and concrete things. Ideas floating inside someone's head don't make a difference.

Most of us think we're doing something good. Most of us think we're making a positive impact. Most of us think we're making the right choice. But if you have all these wonderful intentions without an ounce of action, there's no practical difference between you and anyone else. Intentions can't write your words for you or help you paint a picture.

Here is a list of things that are not actions that move you forward and shouldn't be confused for them:

- Intention
- Observation
- Visualization

- Thinking
- Consumption
- Meditation

For people who tend to have failure to launch, there is often a blurring between intentions and actions. You shouldn't pat yourself on the back and relax just because you've had some thoughts about being productive and working through the night.

After a long day of brainstorming and thinking good thoughts, it's tempting to feel like you've accomplished a lot. But you've accomplished nothing. And you need to recognize this blur to take action. As they say, "The road to hell is paved with good intentions."

Don't assume that just because your intentions are good, you're already making a positive impact. These things are worlds apart. How are you translating your good intentions into something concrete and tangible? What actual steps are you taking to make your hopes reflect reality?

Identify the smallest step you need to take. Think about the biggest goal you have on your agenda. Don't let how ambitious this goal seems or how much work it will take get in your way. It's not that ambitious when you think in terms of small steps. What is the first *small* step you need to do to get this goal rolling? You'll be surprised how easy it is to keep working after you've broken ground. This is the first step in making the leap from mere intention to tangible action.

For example, if you're looking to start brewing your own beer, the first step you need to take is probably studying how the whole process works. There are plenty of books you can buy that describe the process, and even more websites that depict it more succinctly. Maybe your first step is just to clear out enough space in your garage. Those are the first and smallest steps you take before you go out and buy mash, hops, yeast, and jugs that take over your home.

To recognize how you've blurred your intentions and actions and create a separation between them, think in terms of plans. When you have an intention that seems to be masquerading as action, immediately come up with the plan that will bring it to life. Create specific, do-able, and measurable actions that can help ensure you are taking steps.

For example, you might have the intention of achieving more in the workplace. Perhaps you're working for a promotion or you want a raise. Some of us might be tempted to just think about the things we will do better, give ourselves credit for the thought, and pat ourselves on the back without doing a single thing.

Instead, translate that intention into four small, concrete steps that can help you achieve this goal. Even small things like showing up on time or speaking up in meetings can make an impact. These concrete steps will help your good intentions become real, as well as create a sense of accountability to stay on track.

The takeaway here is that too often, we feel that we've already taken action just because we have the intention to. Catch yourself before you fall into that trap, and clearly distinguish between intentions and actual motion.

Important Versus Urgent

A final common mindset mistake is thinking of "important" and "urgent" as synonymous and not realizing the huge gulf between the two terms and how you should prioritize them. The ability to distinguish the two is a key step in taking more action, stopping procrastination, and getting to your end goal with your wits intact.

We spend far too much time on *urgent* tasks when we should be focusing on *important* tasks. What's the difference?

Important task: These contribute directly to our short-term or long-term goals. They are absolutely imperative to our work, responsibilities, or lives. They cannot be skipped and should be prioritized. However, they may not need to be done immediately and thus don't appear to be important. This makes it easy to fall into the trap of ignoring the important for the urgent. But they are what truly impact your various bottom lines, and serious negative repercussions would follow from skipping them.

Urgent task: These simply demand immediacy and speed, and usually come from other people. Of course, this naturally creates a reaction on your end that can make us forget what's important. They *can* overlap with an important task, but they can also just demand your immediate attention without deserving it. These are usually smaller and easier to complete, so often we turn to them out of procrastination, and it allows us to feel quasi-productive even though we've ignored what we *really* need to be doing. Many urgent tasks can be delayed, delegated, or flat-out ignored.

As a quick example, if you are an author under a tight deadline, an *important* task for you would be to continue writing your book. You need to hit 5,000 words a day for the next two weeks or else you are going to be eating bread and oatmeal. This would qualify as a priority.

An *urgent* task would be dealing with that annoying "check engine" light that keeps flickering on and off in your car. Your car can probably survive a few more trips, and even though the winking light can be seductive, you need to resist it, because this is urgent masquerading as important.

Typically, you'll find that an important project might not have that many urgent tasks connected with it. This tends to cause confusion of priorities. Luckily, there is a tried and true method of distinguishing between urgent and important, and the method draws its name from one of the most famous American presidents, Dwight D. Eisenhower. It's called the Eisenhower Matrix, and it will help you identify and prioritize what you really need to be juggling at the moment.

Eisenhower was a five-star general during World War II before being elected president and serving two presidential terms. To master his schedule, Eisenhower developed a system that helped him sort his activities and demands into matters that were most important and identify the most vital processes to serve those crucial elements. It also helped him determine which less-essential tasks he could either designate someone else to complete or eliminate entirely. In other words, important versus urgent.

Eisenhower's matrix is easy for anyone to employ and goes a long way toward improving efficiency and accomplishment. The template is a simple two-by-two grid divided between "important" goals and "urgent" tasks, as seen below.

The Eisenhower Matrix

	Urgent	Not Urgent
Important	DO it today	SCHEDULE a time to do it
Not Important	DELEGATE it to someone else	ELIMINATE Stop doing this

www.expertprogrammanagement.com

Important tasks. The top row of the matrix represents the most important responsibilities one has in their life. These are things that require our most active attention. For work, these might include the most pertinent aspects of our job descriptions—overseeing a budget, managing a long-term project that defines our business, or maintaining constant operations. For personal matters, it could mean maintaining our health (or that of our loved ones), sustaining a relationship or marriage, selling a house, or establishing a business. Whatever things most impact every other thing in our lives or work are the most important.

However, just because something is extremely important doesn't mean every activity that supports it needs to be done immediately. Some can be put on the backburner (indefinitely, even), some aren't ready to be dealt with, and some depend on other people moving first. In short, you can't do them all *right now*. That's where the "urgency" metric comes in: the top row of the matrix is thus divided according to what can happen now and what can be delayed (but must happen at some point in the future).

Urgent: Do. Objects in the "do" quadrant are things that absolutely need to be done posthaste. They must be completed to stave off unfavorable outcomes or uncontrollable circumstances, and the sooner they're done, the less work (and more relief) there will be in the future. "Do" tasks typically revolve around deadlines: final term papers, court filings, car registrations, school applications, and so forth.

They also include emergencies or activities that need to be completed to avert disaster. "Do" tasks are best thought of as duties that need to be finished immediately, by the end of today, or tomorrow at the very latest. They cause anxiety because they're high-effort duties that you dread but need to do nevertheless.

Not urgent: Plan. Tasks that reside in the second quadrant need to be done at some point—but not necessarily *now*. The world isn't going to collapse if they're not done today; they're not on a strict deadline to be completed. Still, they have to be done at *some* point, usually relatively soon, so they need to be scheduled. "Plan" tasks include setting up a future meeting with a big client, arranging a time for a roof leak to be fixed, studying or reading class materials or work documents, or maintenance duties that cover the long term.

Schedule them after the fires are put out. Plan them for the near future, but not so imminent that it interferes with your truly urgent *and* important tasks. "Plan" tasks are also key components of your medium-to-long range plans: when you're planning a week or a month in advance, "plan" tasks should be put on your timetable.

The danger with these "not urgent" tasks is deprioritizing them too much. They're important to keep normal operations afloat, and if they're discarded or forgotten, they may well turn into emergencies in short order. Take the "check engine" light in your car from earlier—anecdotally, I have driven with that light on for close to a year and nothing terrible has happened, so even though it's theoretically important, it doesn't demand urgent attention.

Not-important tasks. The bottom row of Eisenhower's matrix represents tasks that aren't that significant to you personally. That doesn't mean they're unimportant to other people (though it might), but they're activities that might be more appropriate or meaningful for somebody else to finish up. Other people will certainly attempt to present them as important to you, but they're often just projecting their own self-interests. Is there an impact on you? Minimal, if any. The not-important tier is also divided up by relative urgency.

Urgent: Delegate. Perhaps the most befuddling square in this matrix is the "not-important but urgent" box. It perhaps makes the most sense in a work environment: these are tasks that might really need to be done, but it's not vital for *you* to take care of them yourself, even if you could. If you *did* complete them yourself, they might impose on the "important" items that you absolutely have to do either now or later.

For those reasons, items in this box should be eliminated, preferably by being delegated to somebody else. When you're working as the leader of a team, you should be able to find someone else to handle these tasks for you.

Not-important/urgent tasks can be identified by measuring how vital they are to what's happening now. These can very generally be described as interruptions: phone calls, emails, ongoing family situations, and so forth. During times of inactivity these all may be important to focus on, but at the moment they could distract or misdirect you from what you have to accomplish toward your overall goals.

You may be fielding customer support emails even though you are the CEO of the hundred-person company. These customer support emails represent extremely angry and disturbed clients, and they're urgent to everyone involved—except you.

There really is no point or importance for you to be involved in this daily minutia, and thus, you must eliminate it from your schedule through delegation.

Not urgent: Eliminate. Finally, there are some activities and functions that are neither important nor time-sensitive to the priorities at hand. What are they even there for? Mostly to distract you or serve as an escape from doing what you need to do: leisure activity, social media, binge-watching, long phone calls, extensive hobby time, and so forth. In the name of efficiency and prioritizing, these things are dead weight—we might not always be optimizing for those things, but it is still helpful to simply know where your time is going.

These are just elements that grab your attention for one reason or another and try to force a response; they're even hard to name sometimes because they feel so insignificant and fleeting. But they add up. (If you ever want to shock yourself and see how much they add up, install trackers on your phone and computer to see how much time you log on truly useless pursuits.)

These are the activities you shouldn't account for in your schedule at all and should only be done when everything else is completed. Only keep items that are important to the bottom-line success of your project or life. This doesn't mean you can't *ever* do them (and you'd be mistaken not to allow yourself a little bit of escapism now and then). But when you're in the middle of other important items that need your attention or oversight, take these distractions off your plate completely. They'll be more meaningful and rewarding when you've finished the important tasks anyway.

Just because something appears to demand a quick response doesn't mean you should give it, and just because something is slowly ticking in the background doesn't mean you should ignore it. Learn to balance the two for optimal decisions.

Takeaways and action steps:

- As you can tell, taking action is more than something you simply decide to do one day. It's a habit, and ideally will

become part of the mindset with which you approach the world.
- One way to get into this mindset is to approach it from a different angle. Instead of constantly working to take action, you could seek to banish zero days from your life. A zero day is simply a day (or other time period) in which you take no action toward your goals. You just need to be able to say yes or no for a time period to avoid your zero day, and it can be as small an action as you can think of. The point is to build consistency and eventual motivation.
  - Action step: Set up your zero days. Set a specific goal, and promise to do something tangible to further that goal. It doesn't matter how small it is; just make it so no day goes by resulting in zero action. Try to have a string of unbroken days.
- Do you find yourself focused on solutions or problems? As we have often said, you can't think and do at the same time. When you're concentrating on

problems, you're stuck in place and not interested in moving forward. When you're focused on solutions, you're asking the right questions and jumping into motion. If you want to get from Point A to Point B, there is very little room for problem-focused thinking.

- o Action step: Stop asking why. Why doesn't particularly help you formulate a plan to move forward and take action. Instead of fixating on something that is already a fact you can't change, ask yourself questions centered around what you can do first and what you can do now.

- Do you pat yourself on the back just for thinking about taking action? A big pitfall is when intentions and actions blur together. This causes you to be fooled into thinking you've done what you're supposed to do, even though you've done nothing but spin your wheels. Separate these two distinct acts and learn to not feel so satisfied from mere intentions.

- Action step: Whenever you realize you are starting to blur the gap between intentions and actions, think in terms of plans. Take your intention and break it down into four small steps that will make the intention reality. It's important to build a mental separation between these two elements.
- Finally, learn to distinguish between urgent and important tasks. One matters, while the other only appears to because it may have more time constraints. But urgency by itself doesn't denote any kind of priority. To master the difference, try using the Eisenhower Matrix to divide your tasks into four separate categories; you'll find that much less matters than you previously thought. It is similar to the don't-do list because it can create clarity on what you are wasting your time on.
  - Action step: Create an Eisenhower Matrix. Understand what needs to be done, what can be skipped,

and what should be eliminated immediately.

Chapter 4. Maximize Momentum

Success seems to be connected with action. Successful people keep moving. They make mistakes but don't quit. - Conrad Hilton

This is the chapter that assumes you can now occasionally kick your butt into action. You can achieve blastoff sometimes—perhaps not consistently, but you can do it when you put your mind to it. Obviously, this is something we want to improve upon. How can you make it easier to always spring into action when you want?

This is the concept of *momentum*—when you can create less resistance to your first step and make your second and third steps flow easily thereafter. Momentum doesn't necessarily depend on your mindset or thoughts. It actually hinges more upon your environment, your planning, and the ways that you set yourself up for success or failure. It's how you are able to make the right choice time after time. Willpower and self-discipline won't always get you there, but you can design your life to create and maximize momentum.

Banish Your Excuses

People use excuses to postpone taking action. Excuses, on one hand, are our subconscious protecting us from danger, real or imagined. It is your automatic pilot saying, "Danger! This might not go well! Let me save you the embarrassment, failure, and rejection!" They are how we rationalize our way through tough situations.

But on the other hand, most excuses are poppycock—invalid, rubbish, and rationalized. There's no other way to put it, and for the purposes of this book, I wish to be extremely black and white about this.

Almost all of your excuses are lies—either intentional lies or unconscious defense mechanisms. They just enable you to do what you want to do and feel justified about it. This is something I feel strongly about, because even though life is tough and the world throws curveballs at all of us . . . so what? You still have to do what you have to do, regardless. Just because someone else lacks the obstacles you have doesn't excuse you from taking action. This isn't meant to sound insensitive, but is simply an acknowledgment that the world does not care about excuses, so you should wean yourself off them.

Now that I'm off my soapbox, let's look at some common excuses people use to remain out of action. Three in particular plague us.

Now is not the right time. Related variations: *I can't do X until . . . I can't do X unless . . .* Well, that might be true, but there is never a perfect time for anything. There are mediocre times and terrible times, but rarely are there perfect times. Stop putting conditions around your ability to act. All you are doing is creating a psychological gatekeeper for yourself.

Timing is everything—that's actually not true. Timing just *is*. There is no good time for a crisis, but they happen anyway. When trying to be productive, rarely is there an obvious moment that is better than another. It's just a lie we tell ourselves. There are always going to be obstacles to overcome and hassles to manage. In fact, 99 percent of the time you want to do something, the timing will be mediocre, 1 percent, the timing will be truly terrible, and that's it. There should never be any expectations of having perfect timing.

When is the right time to travel? When is the right time to get married? When is the right time to have a child? When is the right time to quit a job, goal, or marriage? You know the answer to these questions—there may be truly *terrible* times, but there exists no perfect time to upend your life in small or large ways.

For instance, there is never an ideal time to sell a house. The housing market is unpredictable, and various rates are subject to change overnight. You also don't know what bids you will receive and if anyone will even view your home. On the other hand, there are some objectively horrible times to sell a house, like when a main employer in town lays off 50 percent of its workforce and interest rates take a 10 percent rise.

Many of us wish timing was something we had more control over, but the fact remains that we rarely get to choose when something happens to us. We do, however, get to decide when we take action. If you find yourself questioning this, the time to act has already arrived.

I don't know where to start. You do; the problem is you think you need an entire plan before starting. You need to stop expecting to clearly see a path through to the end before you even begin; in reality, you just need to identify the first one or two steps. Everything else comes afterward and may even change drastically from what you first imagined. It's the mindset of building a staircase step by step, as you are climbing it, as opposed to constructing it completely before you ever take a single step.

Here is the secret: you don't need to know where you will finish to identify where to start. The number-one college major for students entering university in the US is *undecided*. Most eighteen-year-olds are not able to articulate what they want to study that will lead to a lifelong career. However, we encourage young people to get to college soon after high school. "Don't wait too long. Don't amass too many responsibilities," we say. During the four (or five) years they are on campus, most students declare a major and start working toward a degree that will eventually lead to employment.

We think nothing of this process; however, so many times in adulthood, people become paralyzed because they don't see a clear finish line. Doing something right away with what you have today is the key. Stop researching, stop agonizing, stop wasting time, and start doing. Do what you can do right now at this very moment, and you can figure out the next move after. You probably know your next steps, however small they may be. You don't know the end point, but you absolutely know where to start.

If you set out on a road trip, do you need to know your absolute end destination with a degree of certainty? It helps, but no. You just need to know enough to get you through the first hour or two of driving, and then you can stop along the way and figure it out. What's important is that you began your trip instead of endlessly planning.

The blank page or the blank screen is the writer's nightmare. It does not matter if the writer is a middle schooler with a book report due or Stephen King. The blank page is terrifying. And yet, all who eventually produced something to fill that paper or screen had to stop reading the book, stop researching the topic, stop planning out the flow, and just start writing.

The first words written may not be any good. They may be terrible and need to be changed. But the writer cannot get there if they never write any words down—the first step. Focusing on the end product, a hardback with a glossy cover, isn't the goal at the beginning. A beginning is the goal. After you start, the rest will take care of itself because you will know what needs to be done to get you to the next step, and then the one after that.

I'm not good enough. Shockingly, that just might be true. A person may really want to do something, but they might not be good enough. What is the answer to that dilemma? You can *become* good enough.

Sometimes the only way to get what you want is to shift into a growth mindset and start working. Make sure that this time next year, you know more than you do now and that your skills are better than they are currently. If you are willing to take the first steps, what you need will follow.

When you feel like you are not good enough, you might need to reframe it just a bit to "I'm not good enough *at this moment*." After all, why would anyone have the expectation that they would be good enough at something without practice, work, and a significant amount of time? You simply cannot have the expectation of instant, or even preemptive, excellence. If you never start, you will never be good enough, and you will have prophesized your own failure.

You have to lower your expectations and realize that you probably won't be *good enough* at first, and it might take you a while—but if you never start, there's a 0 percent chance you'll reach adequacy. There's a reason one of the most widespread conceptions of expertise is the 10,000 Hour Rule, first put forth by Anders Ericsson and then popularized by Malcolm Gladwell, which states that you need 10,000 hours of focused practice to become an expert in any field or skill.

Learning a musical instrument is an illustrative example. When people say they aren't musical before picking up an instrument, it makes little sense, doesn't it? If learning to play the piano is your goal, then you can certainly make it happen. You would have to start back at that beginning middle C, but with lessons, practice, patience, and perseverance, anyone, including you, can learn to play the piano. Who knows? Perhaps you could eventually become a keyboard player for a Queen cover band. Just because you are not good enough now does not mean you cannot become proficient eventually. Your lofty expectations shouldn't hold you back from action.

Combating excuses is difficult because of our overwhelming need for self-protection—sometimes we even resort to lying to ourselves. We may not even realize when we are using defense mechanisms to avoid action, but chances are if you find yourself justifying a lack of motion, you're using an excuse, and almost all excuses are lies.

Temptation Bundling

Temptation bundling is a way to kill inaction by, essentially, bribery.

We've mentioned that one reason for a lack of action is a separation between the current you and the future you. You're only thinking about instant gratification, instead of delaying gratification to benefit the future you. Conceived by behavioral psychologist Katy Milkman at the University of Pennsylvania, temptation bundling is a way to blend both future and present needs by making future rewards more immediate. You give yourself instant gratification in the present while also achieving goals that benefit your future self in the long term.

It's good for the current you *and* the future you. And it's simpler than it sounds.

If your goal is to satisfy the two versions of yourself (current and future), think about what that would require. Future self wants you to buckle down and take care of business so they are in a good position, or at least not suffering from your neglect. However, current self wants to engage in hedonism and enjoy the present moment. Think eating Twinkies while working out, working out while watching TV, or doing work while soaking your feet in a salt bath—these are examples of ways to make the long-term feel good at the present moment, and this is the essence of temptation bundling.

Bundle a temptation (current pleasure) with an unpleasurable activity (something you would otherwise procrastinate), and you get the best of both worlds.

There is no need to suffer in the present to get something done for your future self; if you do suffer, then you will lose all motivation and procrastinate. So find ways to bundle your temptations with your long-term goals. In other words, pair your obligations with instantaneous rewards.

Milkman found that up to 51 percent of her study participants were willing to take action when temptation bundling was introduced. It is an effective means to correct procrastination and avoidance habits. To use this for yourself, you should make a list with two columns, one side being your guilty pleasures or temptations and the other being things you need to do for your future self. Then figure out creative ways to link the two conflicting columns in harmony.

Suppose you like chocolate, surfing, and soccer. But work, homework, and piano lessons stand in your way.

Chocolate   Homework
Surfing   Work
Soccer   Piano Lessons

How might you combine things to make the unpleasurable more tolerable? There are at least nine combinations between these elements, and nine different ways you can bundle temptations. How might you combine chocolate with homework, soccer with work, and surfing with piano lessons? It doesn't take long to imagine how you can bribe yourself into doing exactly what you need to do.

Action is usually unpleasant; in the best-case scenarios, it's something we'd rather not be doing. When you can make the unpleasant just a little bit more tolerable, that's a winning formula.

Improve Your Environment

Tinkering with your environment can make action a whole lot easier.

This notion may seem disempowering. We'd prefer to think of success as the result of our own hard work—resolve, effort, and determination. Conversely, we fault failure on deficiencies in willpower, ability, talent, or performance.

But when you study how human behavior evolves over a long time period, environment frequently plays more of a part in success than motivation or skill. Environment is the hidden force that guides human behavior. Yes, incentive, intelligence, and labor are important, but these traits often get overwhelmed by the surroundings in which we dwell. It's as simple as us being more inclined to eat cookies if we have an open bag of cookies right next to us for hours a day.

External factors are the invisible accomplices for shaping how we react and behave. Over time, the environment conditions our actions and habits on a greater scale than our "natures"—our talents and beliefs—do. And it's possible to tweak those surroundings so we're enabled to use our talents, decision-making skills, and efforts in the most action-oriented way possible.

Brian Wansink of Cornell University conducted a study on dietary habits in 2006 and made an interesting discovery. When people switched from serving plates twelve inches in diameter to plates that were ten inches, they wound up eating 22 percent *less* food. This finding was so effective that food writers have recycled it as a tip for diet success, to the extent that some espouse using tiny plates and tiny portions to curb appetites.

It's a great example of how even a minor adjustment in an environment can contribute to improved decision-making. The change in plate size was a minuscule two inches—not quite the width of a smartphone—but yielded more than one-fifth of a decrease in consumption. Repeated over time, this minor modification can build up good habits to make major impacts.

The guiding principle is to make your environment more likely to trigger the action you want to increase and hinder inaction you want to eliminate—and then ensure these triggers fit in the flow of your life. Simply put, use your environment to make it easier to lose your inertia. Make the easy thing the right thing; make it the default thing, even.

For instance, if you want more incentive to practice a musical instrument, you could make a permanent place for the instrument in the middle of a room with instructions of exactly where to pick up. You could also leave a trail of sheet music that literally requires you to pick it up to walk to your bed. If you want to work out more, you're more likely to visit a gym if it's located on your way home from work, rather than ten miles in the opposite direction.

You can also put your gym bag in front of your front door, buy a pull-up bar for your kitchen doorway, and only wear shoes that can double as exercise shoes. Finally, if you want to procrastinate less, you can leave reminder Post-its next to door handles and your wallet (things you will have to touch), leave your work in a place you can't avoid it, and hide your distracting temptations.

Decreasing inaction is a function of *out of sight, out of mind*. For example, supermarkets often place higher-priced items at customers' eye levels to increase the chances they'll buy them. But one could *reverse* this process at home by keeping unhealthy foods away from immediate view and storing them in less visible or harder-to-reach levels. Put your chocolate inside five containers like a Russian nesting doll and put them in a closet—see how often you binge then.

To stop smoking, one might consider removing all the ashtrays from inside the home and placing them as far away as possible on the perimeter of their property so smoking will necessitate a brisk walk in the freezing winter. To keep from sitting down all day, you can switch to a standing desk that will force you to stand up during most working hours. You could also simply remove chairs and coffee tables from the area in which you do most of your work.

The whole idea is to eliminate having to make decisions, because that's where we usually hit a snag. Depending on willpower and discipline is risky to say the least, so create an environment that will help you automate your decisions toward action. In taking that choice out of your hands, you're rewiring yourself to eliminate bad habits from your routine—and likely saving a little time in the process.

Author Mihaly Csikszentmihalyi, known for the book *Flow*, calls this general approach for environment changing one's *activation energy*—the less activation energy required to make good decisions and take action, the better. And by contrast, the higher the activation energy for staying in inaction, the better. Activation energy can also be seen as the overall amount of effort people are willing to spend. Make the conscious choice to make action more immediately accessible, and action has a better chance of becoming a permanent lifestyle change.

The If-Then Technique

This method is a surefire way to stick to your good intentions toward action and actually translate them into real life no matter what's thrown at you. It's also extremely simple. While considering your desired action, simply replace the italics in this phrase: "If *event occurs*, then *your action*." We can think of this method in three steps.

First, choose a goal that you want to accomplish.

Second, create a list of the actions your goal needs to succeed but that you are likely to avoid.

Third, tie the action to something that is unavoidable in your daily life. You can think about this in terms of linking actions to each other with the intent that they eventually become one big activity in your mind. And obviously, you want it to be connected to something that will occur frequently, and definitively.

For instance, suppose that your overall goal is improving your fitness level: Tell yourself "if you brush your teeth, then you will do ten pushups," or "if you put your shoes on, you will walk up and down your street twice for some activity."

If you have the overall goal of practicing the violin more, how might this apply? In the same way: "If you pick up your violin, then you will play three songs minimum," or "if you brush your teeth, then you will practice violin afterward."

If you sit down at your computer, then you will write down two sentences in your book manuscript. If you check your email, then you will reply to at least five emails. Again, you want to tie your goal to something you will consistently do so it becomes habitual for you to take action as well.

You're creating a rule for yourself to abide by, and one of the keys to adherence is that you do it before you have to think about it. If you've given it thought beforehand, you can default to that guideline and not have to try to make a risky decision in the heat of the moment. Remember, it's only when we are given time and space to make poor decisions that we will. The if-then method takes that process out of your hands and makes it less of a choice. Anticipate what's to happen, set a rule, and you will be a step ahead of the game.

Single-tasking

To maximize momentum and begin to take action more often than not, multitasking must become your sworn enemy. But you already knew this. This is similar to what we discussed earlier on motion for motion's sake versus intentional, focused action toward a goal.

The only being who would be great at multitasking is an octopus with two heads. As in, to multitask effectively, one literally needs two brains and eight hands. It's just not within human capability to multitask successfully, no matter what you think or have been told. You simply can't do more than one thing efficiently at a time, so don't try to split your minutes in different directions. You can either do one thing well, or you can do three things very poorly.

Let's take Bob. Bob is on the phone, on his tablet, and on a computer. He gets an e-mail that seems urgent, so he starts to answer it while he's still talking on the phone. He completely loses track of the phone conversation, and he'll have to re-read the report he pulled up on his computer to understand it. It only took one call or e-mail to completely throw Bob off-track and cause all of the things he was juggling to fall out of the air and land on his head. Any action he would have been able to take is now completely wasted, and hours later, he's still at square one. It's ironic that too much action can leave you with none at all, while also consuming your valuable energy stores.

By multitasking, the only thing you will achieve is that you will end up continually distracting yourself, because your mind is focused on too many things to process them all equally and efficiently. According to a study in the *New York Times*, it can take up to twenty-five minutes to regain focus after being distracted. That's twenty-five minutes you will waste trying to find your place and get into the right mindset again.

In 2009, Sophie Leroy published a paper aptly titled "Why is it So Hard to Do My Work?" In it, she explained an effect that she called "attention residue."

Leroy noted that other researchers had studied the effect of multitasking on performance, but that in the modern work environment, once you reached a high enough level, it was more common to find people working on multiple projects sequentially. "Going from one meeting to the next, starting to work on one project and soon after having to transition to another is just part of life in organizations," Leroy explains.

This is essentially the modern version of multitasking—working on projects in short bursts and switching between them, not necessarily doing them all at once. People may not actually be working on multiple tasks at the same time, but it's nearly as bad to keep shifting between them in relatively quick succession.

The problem identified by this research is that you cannot switch seamlessly between tasks without a delay of sorts. When you switch from Task A to Task B, your attention doesn't immediately follow—a residue of your focus remains stuck thinking about the original task. This becomes worse, and the residue becomes especially "thick" if your work on Task A was unbounded and of low intensity before you switched, but even if you finish Task A before moving on, your attention remains divided for a while. Leroy's results were clear: "People experiencing attention residue after switching tasks are likely to demonstrate poor performance on that next task," and the more intense the residue, the worse the performance.

We've all experienced that frantic moment when we're doing too many things at once and suddenly find ourselves unable to do any at all. Even though you are taking the purpose of this book to heart, you are suddenly stuck with the opposite.

How can you concentrate on any task if you keep switching back and forth between two or more different things? You'll likely be stuck simply trying to make sense of everything and organize it so you can understand it. It will only force you to waste time trying to catch up to where you were instead of pushing forward. You'll take one step forward but two steps back each time you try.

There might be certain ways you can multitask 1 percent more effectively, but the overall lesson is just to avoid it whenever possible. Action requires a degree of focus and care, and multitasking is oxymoronic with those things. The answer to this problem is *single-tasking*. What does this mean? To set everything else aside and not check, monitor, e-mail, or even touch anything other than the current task you are working on. It requires singular focus and the purposeful and intentional tuning out of everything else. Switch off your notifications and ditch your phone. If you must be on your computer, keep only one browser tab or program open at a time. Put yourself into a vacuum; if you grow bored or want to procrastinate, there's only one thing for you to do to exit the vacuum.

A lot of single-tasking is about consciously avoiding distractions that seem small and harmless. The biggest culprits? Your electronic devices. Ignore them when possible. Keep a spotless workspace so your eye doesn't catch something that needs cleaning or adjusting. Ideally, single-tasking reduces your environment to a blank room because you shouldn't pay attention to any of it. Out of sight, out of mind.

Attempt to take note of when you are being interrupted or subtly switching between tasks. This is hard to catch at first and will require you to make conscious decisions against your instincts.

Something that will be very hard to resist is the compulsion to tell yourself that you must act on something immediately and interrupt your task. Remember, don't confuse urgent with important. Matters and people alike all want to masquerade as important.

To combat this urge, set aside a notebook to take notes of ideas that will inevitably spring to mind regarding other tasks. Call this your *distraction list*. Just jot them down quickly and return to your primary goal. Whatever they're about, whether it's something that needs to be taken care of or something new and creative that pops into your head, take note but don't act on them right when they come. Don't chase random thoughts, which are the mental equivalent of shiny objects.

Some of these might make their way into your to-do list, but most will probably end up on the don't-do list. You can address them after your single-tasking period is over, and you won't have forgotten anything. This tactic will keep your mind focused on one single task while setting you up for future success.

If you want to accomplish something, do it with 100 percent concentration and focus; otherwise, you might just end up in a worse position than when you started.

25 Minutes at a Time

A practice that can help you push past inertia and into action is the *Pomodoro Technique*. It uncovers that much of the reason we forgo action is not necessarily because we can't get started, but because we cannot remain on task. This tactic concerns continuing along our path and using momentum, rather than starting from ground zero. And of course it ties in nicely with the concept of single-tasking and only paying attention to what's in front of you.

The Pomodoro Technique was invented in the 1990s by an author named Francesco Cirillo. He discovered that if he broke his work schedule down into short sections he timed with his tomato-shaped timer, his ability to focus on his work improved. Over time, he even found that his attention span lengthened and his capacity to concentrate on single projects over a longer period of time grew stronger.

More than that, the timed and scheduled system of working reminded him to take regular breaks, which increased his motivation to work and improved his ability to solve problems creatively. He named his new technique *pomodoro*, after the timer that facilitated the whole process.

If you also want to enhance your productivity, increase your attention, and improve your concentration while taking time to relax and recuperate, the Pomodoro Technique could be perfect for you. Here's how you do it:

First, choose a task to complete. If you have several tasks, or your project is very long and complex, you will need to break your work into smaller portions that can be completed within twenty-five minutes. For example, if you want to read a book, you can divide it into twenty-five-minute sections based on your reading speed, perhaps slightly more than you think you can fit in. You can always keep working after the timer goes off, but if you run out of things to do during a pomodoro, you won't be able to complete the unit uninterrupted. You don't want that!

Second, set your timer to twenty-five minutes. This will define the length of time you'll be working without any breaks or interruptions.

Third, work, study, or learn until the timer rings. Once it rings, you can put a check mark or a sticker onto a piece of paper so that you know how many pomodoros you've managed to complete in a single day. This lets you track your progress and really see how much time you've dedicated to your project.

Fourth, take a short break. Five minutes is a good period of time for a break, but it doesn't have to be exact. The whole point is to rest, stretch, and get yourself into good shape for another pomodoro. Keep it short!

When you're done with a pomodoro, you can watch a YouTube video, go for a walk, or get a cup of water, tea, or coffee. Getting up, moving around, and relaxing your mind is the order of the day. But don't get too far off track, and don't you dare engage in anything that will take longer than five minutes.

Fifth, after every four pomodoros, take a longer break. This break can last between fifteen and twenty-five minutes, but should be as long as you need to rest, recuperate, and feel fresh and ready to start another pomodoro. This is your chance to really unwind for a bit; stretch your mental muscles, but know that you are probably in for another set of four pomodoros.

During your longer breaks, you can read about something else, spend time on your favorite social media sites, or even take a power nap. With a longer break, you have even more options for your own enjoyment. And after four pomodoros, you can do it guilt-free, because you've already done a good amount of studying or learning that day.

An essential aspect of this action method is that a pomodoro is an inviolable, indivisible period of work. You can't start your timer, get distracted, and count the time you weren't working as a valid pomodoro. If you're interrupted or discover yourself spacing out, you have to stop your pomodoro and restart it when you're ready to begin again. The whole point of the method is to train yourself to be productive and to focus for twenty-five whole minutes; if you fail, you start again until your brain gets used to the rhythm. Sooner or later, you will become accustomed to the pace, and it'll be a lot easier to focus and pound out work for the entire pomodoro.

Interruptions from other people are harder to control, but Cirillo teaches a method to overcome that possibility, too. His advice is to follow the "inform, negotiate, call back" method to handle untimely interruptions. Using it involves a four-step process. This is similar to the distraction list you would create when single-tasking.

First, inform the person who approaches you that you're busy right now and can't interrupt your work at the moment.

Second, negotiate when you can get back to them so they know you aren't going to ignore their needs.

Third, schedule a follow-up. Setting a specific time to get back to them will reassure them and make them more likely to leave you to your pomodoro.

Fourth and finally, call them back when your pomodoro is complete. Because you rescheduled their interruption, it becomes your responsibility to get back to them and engage with their needs.

Remember, despite the strict need to continue pomodoros for the entire twenty-five minutes, they're not a prison sentence. You are free to continue work past the twenty-five-minute timer as long as you remember to take a break once the chunk of work you chose to do is finished. Breaks also increase productivity by keeping you refreshed and ready for work at all hours of the day. Work, then rest.

After you've trained with the Pomodoro Technique for a while, it's possible to increase your attention span and improve your concentration even further by doubling the timespan into the *50-10 rule*. This encourages you to set your study and productivity timer to fifty instead of twenty-five minutes, and lets you take a break twice as long once you finish. The benefit of this is that you're resting, recuperating and pursuing other interests just as much, but your ability to focus and be productive should be even more finely honed. Being able to do more for longer, without needing to take a break or being distracted by interruptions, is always a good thing. However, you'll probably have to work up to this.

When the 50-10 rule becomes easy and manageable, you can push yourself one step further into the *60-60-30 method*.

The 60-60-30 method involves working for sixty minutes twice, and then resting for thirty minutes. More specifically, it suggests using two iterations of the 50-10 method back to back, and then following those two sessions with resting for thirty minutes. Setting a timer when you work and rest allows you to avoid looking at the clock, and at this point, working or studying for fifty minutes straight should feel fairly natural. This method just amps up the process further while reminding you to stay refreshed and rested as you're getting stuff done.

Overall, it should be clear why these methods of focusing are successful at battling your short attention span.

Takeaways and action steps:

- One of the best ways to gain and keep momentum is to deal with your excuses. I'm sorry to break it to you, but almost all of them are fake. They are either intentional or unconscious lies. The main culprits are: "I'm not good enough," "I don't know where to start," and "now is not the right time."
    - Action step: For something you are trying to avoid right now, list out a few excuses. Are they real excuses, or are they just explanations for why something is difficult? There is a very large difference between the two.
- Temptation bundling is the act of blending instant gratification (inaction) and delayed gratification (action). Basically, you bribe yourself by pairing action with rewards—that way, both the

current you and the future you are satisfied.
- o Action step: Create a list of the actions you have been avoiding, and add a list of bribes or rewards that you can tie to each action. For instance, practicing the piano gets you a piece of chocolate. Create your own pairings to experience the benefits of temptation bundling.
- Your environment might be one of the most underappreciated aspects of changing your behaviors and mindset. The human brain operates on what it sees and what surrounds it, so you must curate your environment to help you be action-oriented. You can do this by making the easy thing the right thing. Think about how you can remove your willpower from the equation.
  - o Action step: Take at least three steps in curating your environment to make taking action almost effortless. This can be putting things into your

path, removing distractions, or even placing reminders everywhere.
- The if-then technique is a way of chaining behaviors together. You link a normal, everyday behavior with a goal-oriented action. This sounds fancy, but you are just trying to create a habit out of something unpleasurable. The magic is in the pre-decision and making a rule for yourself before you must make a decision.
    - Action step: Just like with temptation bundling, list out a set of everyday behaviors, such as brushing teeth, and create a separate list of actions that move you toward your goal. Pair them so that every time your everyday activity occurs, you take action toward your goal.
- Multitasking is a big, fat myth. You probably have the best of intentions with it—after all, multitasking is an excess of action. But too much action will sadly leave you with no action, as

you won't be able to focus and truly progress. The key to beating this is single-tasking and 100 percent concentration and commitment to one task at a time.

- Action step: Realize that modern multitasking is actually switching between tasks in a short amount of time. This doesn't work well because of attention residue. So go to your calendar or planner and block off larger amounts of time devoted to one task only. Have a distraction list ready to jot down thoughts that would otherwise derail you during your single-tasking session. Understand that even without constant attention, the world outside of your task will not fall apart.

- The Pomodoro Technique helps keep you on track and on task, rather than getting you up from ground zero. A pomodoro consists of twenty-five

minutes of focused, uninterrupted work, followed by five minutes break. Rinse and repeat as many cycles as you can. It's possible to build up to intervals of fifty minutes and ten minutes, or even sixty minutes, sixty minutes, and then thirty minutes for a break.
- o Action step: Do this now. Not much else to say about this one.

Chapter 5. Beating Procrastination

Many great ideas go unexecuted, and many great executioners are without ideas. One without the other is worthless. - Tim Blixseth

You may not have realized how deeply it has seeped into your daily behaviors and habits, and now this avoidance of action is holding you back from the rest of your life. For most of us, procrastination is the big obstacle to getting into motion.

The term "procrastination" was derived from the Latin words *pro*, meaning "forward, forth, or in favor of," and *crastinus*, meaning "of tomorrow." Its literal translation can thus be taken to be the moving forward of something to tomorrow, or favoring tomorrow as the ideal time. It's never today, always another moment to be later determined.

Procrastination is the act or habit of putting something off until a future time. It involves delaying what needs to be done, usually because the task is unpleasant or boring—or simply because delaying is an option. Rationality isn't involved in procrastinating; in fact, we use rationality far less on a daily basis than we would like to think. And thus, we find ourselves in a hole of our own digging.

Note that procrastination deals only with intended tasks (i.e. tasks you should be doing), and not *all the other tasks* open for you to do. For instance, delaying working on the sales report you're expected to hand in by the end of the week is procrastinating, but putting off all other tasks you don't intend to do—say, go around the community helping Girl Scouts sell Thin Mints—isn't. The defining feature of procrastination is that it involves pushing back tasks you know are better off completed now. It is essentially an act of avoiding discomfort (i.e. the trouble of doing the intended task) and pursuing pleasure instead (i.e. substituting more enjoyable activities, plus the relief of not having to engage in the intended task). Who needs help with pursuing pleasure, after all?

Since the time of ancient civilizations, our ancestors have struggled with the dilemma of choosing to do what needs to be done over other, usually more pleasant, activities. We may imagine that our less industrious forebears must have had days when they relaxed lying under the shade of a tree instead of picking up their spears to hunt or their baskets to forage for food. Hesiod, a Greek poet who lived around 800 BC, cautioned not to "put your work off till tomorrow and the day after." Roman consul Cicero was also an early dissenter against procrastination, calling the act "hateful" in the conduct of affairs. This is clearly a problem that is older than we give it credit for.

So if avoidance and procrastination have been around since time immemorial, where did the impulse for this habit come from? Has it been hardwired in our brains from the beginning?

Neurobiologists have found evidence that *yes*, the fundamental workings of our brains might indeed offer a recipe for procrastination. Remember that procrastination is the act of delaying an intended important task despite knowing there will be negative consequences as a result. In other words, we have no problem recognizing that procrastination is bad for us. In fact, we rationally know it's something to avoid at all costs. Procrastination is thus a failure of self-regulation.

Experts say we procrastinate because we're not that adept at keeping firm command over our capricious drives and impulses—and here's where neurobiologists lay out for the rest of us the biological basis of why we procrastinate.

Imagine the brain as having two major portions—one inner portion and one outer portion. Now, the inner portion is what some scientists call our "lizard brain," responsible for our most basic survival instincts. This region is fully developed from birth and controls our most primitive drives (e.g. hunger, thirst, and sex drive), as well as our mood and emotions (e.g. fear, anger, and pleasure). It's one of the most dominant portions of our brain, as its processes tend to be automatic, not to mention life-maintaining. This section is called the limbic system. It quite literally keeps us alive because we don't have to consciously think about breathing or becoming hungry; it just happens and we live to see another day.

The brain's outer portion, enclosing the limbic system and situated just behind our forehead, is called the prefrontal cortex. While the limbic system has been dubbed as our "lizard brain," the prefrontal cortex has been identified by neurobiologists as the portion that separates us humans from lesser animals. The prefrontal cortex is in charge of our rational human functions, such as assimilating information, planning, making decisions, and other higher-order thinking skills.

So while the limbic system lets us experience instincts and emotions automatically, the prefrontal cortex requires us to put in conscious and deliberate effort to think, plan, decide, and ultimately compete a task. The prefrontal cortex works much, much slower, and we are generally conscious of these thoughts.

By now, you may recognize how these two major portions of the brain must be continuously engaged in battle, a battle you feel most intensely when you're faced with something you would rather not do but have to. In instances such as these, your limbic system is screaming, "*Don't do it! It doesn't feel good!*" while your prefrontal cortex is trying to reason with you: "*You have to do this.*"

It might sound like a cop out, however, to just point fingers at our inherent biology. After all, all humans possess the same brain structure, so there must be some differentiation between those who act and those who do not. To this end, researcher Laura Rabin of Brooklyn College delved into a closer examination of the relationship between procrastination and what are known as the executive functions, which include planning, problem-solving, and self-control.

9 Subscales of Failure

Rabin's study assessed a sample of 212 students for procrastination, as well as the nine clinical subscales of executive functioning: (1) inhibition, (2) self-monitoring, (3) planning and organization, (4) activity shifting, (5) task initiation, (6) task monitoring, (7) emotional control, (8) working memory, and (9) general orderliness.

The researchers expected the first four of these subscales to be linked to procrastination. As it turned out, the results exceeded their expectations—all nine subscales were found to have significant associations with procrastination, as reported by Rabin in a 2011 issue of the *Journal of Clinical and Experimental Neuropsychology*. Let's consider how each of these nine executive functions relates to procrastination and sabotages your ability to act. This chapter will focus primarily on these nine factors and how they keep you standing still.

Inhibition. This pertains to your ability to be "in control" of yourself, to resist impulses, and to stop your own behavior when it's appropriate to do so. Inability to perform this function well leads to impulsivity, which typically manifests as acting without thinking. If you're prone to acting without first considering the consequences of your actions, then you might have problems with inhibition.

Lack of inhibition is a key factor in procrastination. If you can't control yourself enough to resist the impulse of going for an easier, more pleasurable activity, then you'll always choose to do virtually anything else other than what you're supposed to be doing. You'll always be giving in to the temptation to engage in a more enjoyable activity, rather than taking the pains of sticking to your to-do list.

Say you've intended to spend your first hour at the office researching ideas for your marketing proposal. However, as you sit down to work on it, your phone keeps beeping with notifications from the lively social media scene. Lacking inhibitory control, you fail to resist checking your phone and engaging with your friends on social media, and thus you end up procrastinating on your intended research task.

Self-monitoring. This refers to your ability to monitor your own behavior and its effect on yourself and others. It involves a sense of social or interpersonal awareness, such that you not only recognize how you behave, but you also understand why people react the way they do toward you. If this quality is impaired, you might have trouble perceiving both your progress and your delays, and you'll likely always be questioning why certain people treat you the way they do.

Inability to self-monitor thus inevitably results in a severe lack of self-awareness. It means you can't think about your own thinking, and thus you can be ruled by your lizard brain without even being aware of it. When lacking such self-awareness and the ability to analyze your thinking, you'll be more likely to fall prey to destructive patterns of thought and bad habits, including procrastination.

Inadequate self-monitoring is thus linked with procrastination. When you're unaware of how you behave, you're less likely to even realize you're procrastinating. What's more, when you fail to recognize how your behavior impacts others, you'll experience less pressure to deliver on your commitments, which means you'll feel freer to put off tasks till a later time. Lack of self-monitoring will not only lead you to procrastinate, but also hinder you from taking steps to address it.

For instance, imagine you're set to update employee records one afternoon because an independent audit is coming up. However, instead of getting to the task, you get caught up in a conversation with your boss about the importance of keeping updated files. You feel there's nothing wrong with keeping the conversation going; after all, your discussion is relevant to the project. You fail to see that this very conversation is precluding you from actually doing the very task you're supposed to be completing. You're procrastinating, and you don't even realize it.

Planning and organization. This comprises your ability to manage present and future task demands. The planning component of this function is about your capacity to set goals and map out the right order of steps to get the job done. The organization element pertains to your ability to pick up on the main ideas of a given information load and to bring order to information. Together, planning and organization involve your ability to accurately anticipate future situations and demands, and to take those into account as you lay out the steps necessary to achieve your goals.

Insufficient planning and organization is related to procrastination. If you lack the ability to set realistic goals and establish plans to meet those goals, you'll likely miss appreciating how much time you really have to accomplish your intended tasks. Thus, you'll feel at greater liberty to squander time procrastinating rather than getting to work.

Also, if you lack the skills to organize information, you'll likely fixate on irrelevant details of a project rather than work on the major stuff. The worst part about this is you won't feel like you're procrastinating because you'll think you're "working." In reality, though, you're dodging the real job while working on extraneous little tasks to cover up your avoidance.

As an example, imagine you need to work on completing a financial report due two weeks from now. Lacking effective planning skills, you don't break down the task into smaller portions and don't set specific hours you're going to work on it. You simply go through the days doing whatever's pushed under your nose (fonts, formatting, and type of paper to print on) and relaxing when nothing's due on that day. You put off doing the report until you realize, much to your panic, that it's due in two hours' time.

Activity shifting. This reflects your ability to easily move from one activity to another, depending on the demands of the situation. If you're adept at activity shifting, you can make transitions effortlessly and tolerate change. This function also involves your capacity to switch or alternate your attention as needed, and to shift your focus from one aspect of a problem to another. Consider this your ability to be flexible, in terms of both behavior and thinking.

A deficit in activity-shifting ability is linked with procrastination. After all, getting down to work basically constitutes a shift from non-working to working mode. If you're unable to transfer from rest mode or from one productive mode to another, then you'll end up procrastinating because you just can't get yourself to switch to the other side. You'll stagnate at your original state, either doing nothing or continuing an activity you're not supposed to be doing at the time.

Say you've been diligent enough to draw up a schedule for the day. You've written that you're going to do some gardening from 8:00 a.m. to 9:00 a.m., and then move inside the house and work on a manuscript from 9:00 a.m. to 11:00 a.m. However, you're fully enjoying and so engrossed in your gardening that you continue with it well past the time you've set for it to stop.

You end up spending your entire morning just gardening because you lacked the ability to shift your focus and energy onto the next task as scheduled. This form of procrastination can be tricky to spot and address, as it can look like you're making good use of your time when in fact, you're not.

Task initiation. This pertains to your ability to simply start and get going on tasks or activities. It is what enables you to break the inertia of inactivity and take the first step on the task at hand—or on any task, for that matter. The first step is always the toughest. Task initiation also includes your capacity to generate ideas and problem-solving strategies by yourself. If this function is weak, you'll find it very difficult to begin tasks or generate problem-solving approaches. It will feel like you can see a long, winding road stretching out before you, but you just can't lift your foot to take the first step and walk along it.

Problems in task initiation are related to procrastination. You find it difficult to start doing what you should be doing; instead, you continue engaging in other activities you find more enjoyable. You set a "start time" for each of your intended tasks, but once that moment arrives, you always find a reason to reschedule the start time to a later moment.

Consider the following scenario: You need to prepare PowerPoint slides for a sales presentation. It's 8:30 a.m. You say, *"I'll start at 9:00 a.m.,"* and then you do other random, mindless things, supposedly to prep you for the busy day ahead. When you look back at the clock, you see it's 9:15 a.m. So you figure, *"Nah, I'll start at 10:00 a.m."* Sure, you may call it your "perfectionist self just wanting to start things right," but you know what the real problem here is—you just can't find it in you to begin.

Task monitoring. This refers to your ability to evaluate and keep track of your projects, as well as to identify and correct mistakes in your work. This also includes your capacity to judge how easy or difficult a task will be for you and whether your problem-solving approaches are working. If your task-monitoring function is impaired, you'll likely find it difficult to weed out which tasks need to be done first, or you may forget what you need to do altogether.

Deficient task monitoring is associated with procrastination. If you lack the ability to track your tasks, you'll fail to prioritize your activities properly, leading you to focus on the less important stuff. What's more, if you misjudge the difficulty of a certain obligation, you're more likely to put it off until later because you expect it to be easier than it actually is. A more realistic evaluation of the time and effort a task requires is essential to avoiding procrastination.

For instance, say you have a bunch of supply requests to review and approve. You estimate that it will take about an hour to finish all of them, and you've scheduled yourself to do the task during your last hour in the office. However, when that hour arrives, you don't feel motivated to proceed, so you put it off until tomorrow. After all, it will only take an hour.

Eventually, your attention is called, as you've delayed the task for several days already and more work is piling up. When you finally sit down to work, you realize you've underestimated the time it takes to complete the project and regret all the time you wasted procrastinating.

Emotional control. This encompasses your ability to modulate or regulate your emotional responses. When your emotional control function is on point, you're able to react to events and situations appropriately. On the other hand, when your emotional control is problematic, you're likely to overreact to small problems, have sudden or frequent mood changes, get emotional easily, or experience inappropriate outbursts.

Such inability to control your emotions is also likely to negatively impact control of your thoughts. Emotions that run wild can derail the train of thought of even the most rational and intelligent people. So if you can't keep a lid on your emotions, you can't expect to be in full control of your thoughts—and your resulting actions—as well.

Problems with emotional control are related to procrastination. Remember the limbic system, that part of your brain that plays a significant role in your emotions, drives, and instincts? You're practically handing it the reins to direct your behavior if your prefrontal cortex lacks the ability to control your emotional responses.

Imagine how a baby behaves. Because it's not yet adept at emotional control, it mostly just responds to the whims of the limbic system (e.g., when it's hungry, it cries without regard for appropriateness of time and place). Likewise, if you're not adept at emotional control, you too will simply behave as you wish, aiming to reduce pain and increase pleasure at every moment.

Let's say you're trying to work out solutions for a financial problem at the company. This undertaking is important but is causing you so much mental fatigue and distress that you decide to set it aside and pick up that entertaining phone of yours instead. The result? Procrastination.

Working memory. This comprises your capacity to hold information in your mind long enough to be able to complete a task. Your working memory is what enables you to follow complex instructions, manipulate information in your mind (e.g., do mental calculations), and carry out activities that have multiple steps. If you've ever walked into a room and forgotten what you went there for, you've experienced a lapse in your working memory. Scientists and researchers routinely estimate average working memory at having a capacity of *seven, plus or minus two items.*

There's an apparent link between working memory and procrastination. See, working memory is what allows you to recall instructions and keep track of what you're doing. Problems in working memory can arise in two different ways. For some, working memory can be impaired by the presence of temptations and distractions in the environment, such as when an attractive ad pops up while you're doing serious research, stealing your attention away from your task.

For others, their working memory can simply be deficient, such as when they lose track of the information they're currently processing for seemingly no reason at all. For these people, their working memory just doesn't work, and so they're less likely to keep at tasks and more likely to procrastinate instead.

Either way, if your working memory is impaired, then you'll be prone to going off-task instead of focusing on what you need to do. You may have difficulty maintaining your attention on tasks that have multiple steps, leading you to stop halfway through and procrastinate instead.

Say you're tasked to review records of your project expenditures and prepare a progress report to inform upper management of your current project status. You had no problem getting yourself started on the task, but after looking over a couple of financial reports, you're finding it hard to keep track of the connections between all the papers you've been reading. Unable to remain focused, you shift your attention to the office chatter happening at the next cubicle. The next thing you know, you've joined your coworkers' conversation and have successfully abandoned your task for the day.

General orderliness. This refers to your ability to keep the items you need for projects well-organized and readily available, as well as to keep your workspaces orderly so that you're able to find whatever you need when you need it. General orderliness brings efficiency in the way you work, as it allows you to spend less time looking for things and more time actually working on the task.

Lack of general orderliness is associated with procrastination. If your work area or living space is not well-organized, you'll be more likely to find yourself in situations where you need to get up from working and look for things, or even go out and buy materials you forgot you needed. You'll have veritable invitations to procrastinate staring you in the face every moment of the day.

Distracted by these additional activities, you'll be more tempted to delay what you should be doing and instead engage in trivial actions. This applies even to the organization of files in your computer. If in your attempt to find one document, you need to sift through piles of folders with no discernable organizational scheme to them whatsoever, you're likely to come across other stuff that will distract you and lead you to procrastinate.

For instance, say you've sat down to create a module for a staff-training session. After jotting down a few ideas, you realize you need to consult the company manual for certain considerations. So you get up to retrieve said manual, and on your way, you bump into another colleague, whom you end up chatting with over coffee at the pantry. After losing about an hour to that, you manage to get back to your desk to try to work on the module again. You remember you have a computer file of an old module that you can use for reference, so you browse your folders looking for it. As you open folder after folder, you come across one bearing interesting articles you've saved for some light reading. You start reading one, and then another, and another. Procrastination wins again.

In summary, procrastination may arise from problems in each of the nine executive functions—(1) inhibition, (2) self-monitoring, (3) planning and organization, (4) activity shifting, (5) task initiation, (6) task monitoring, (7) emotional control, (8) working memory, and (9) general orderliness.

But there's one more significant barrier to action that is only tangentially related to what we've discussed so far: being too ego-focused versus task-focused.

Task Versus Ego Orientation

When it comes to beating procrastination, taking efficient action or motivating yourself toward your goals, there are a few psychological strategies that can help you get there faster. You may not realize it, but the attitude or approach you take to your goals may in fact be impeding you from achieving them.

Not all goals are created the same, and the perspective we take on the path toward those goals can make a massive difference in whether they are ever realized. Basically, there are two main tactics: having an *ego orientation*, and having a *task orientation*. Though neither is intrinsically better than the other, the fact is that if you value your productivity, your ongoing learning and ultimately achieving what you want, one orientation is going to get you there quicker. So for our purposes, one is better: task orientation.

You can either focus on your actual efforts to achieve the task in front of you (task orientation) or you can focus on comparing yourself to others, i.e. thinking of achievement in terms of your own self-worth relative to others (ego orientation). Outlining these effects is a theory called Achievement Goal Theory, and research consistently determines that task involvement is associated with good mental health and better outcomes, whereas ego orientation is associated with an overall negative outcome. We can think about it from a bird's-eye view by comparing two people. Who will stand a better chance of taking more action: Jim, who is focused on completing a task, or Bob, who is focused on what others think about him? The answer seems obvious, but it's a simple trap that we easily fall into.

Let's look at task orientation first.

This mindset is all about mastering the skill or task at hand. It's the work, the lesson to be learned, the team, the Big Idea. With more practice, we gain mastery in our skill, no matter the field. Essentially, we are *intrinsically* motivated, comparing ourselves to ourselves. It's about improvement, progress, and completion. The pleasure is in the act of doing. Being completely task focused can bring us into "the zone," where we can be completely engrossed in our work, concentrating on the mission without any self-consciousness, driven by the need to explore, understand, create or communicate.

When you are oriented this way toward your goals, you can focus on putting plenty of effort into achieving your aims. You do your best, and may even enjoy pushing yourself. You easily collaborate with teammates, not seeing them as competition but rather eagerly exploring all the ways they can contribute to the project. Hierarchies and protocols are less important here—what you are focused on is the task itself!

Perhaps it goes without saying, but those fully identified with this frame of mind find it far easier to actually enjoy their work. They seem to tire less easily, act more spontaneously and produce better results all around. What's more, a person whose self-concept is not unhealthily tied up in the outcome of their work will not feel foolish for making mistakes, and will not make more mistakes in trying to avoid "uncomfortable" feelings such as not knowing the answer.

However, there is another way to approach the work, and it's with a focus on demonstrating one's own superiority. The ego orientation sees the task at hand as a means to an end—and the end is to enjoy being perceived as competent by others, or more competent compared to others. This is an external source of motivation, as the feeling of mastery is not coming from the individual's own sense of development and learning, but from the external sensation of beating out competitors and being perceived as capable. And if a person acting on ego orientation doesn't feel that their ego will perform well, then there appears to be little reason to act and risk embarrassment.

A person operating from an ego orientation is not primarily inspired by mastering the task itself. They may compare themselves to others and rank their performance on this basis, putting emphasis on winning and being the best rather than doing the job well. Genuine development and mastery are only appreciated if they are in service of winning accolades, being externally praised, or feeling as though one has outperformed compared to others. In other words, it's all about *extrinsic* motivation.

The irony is that although many of us may be drawn to particular goals because of this ego element, it's this very attitude that most undermines our ability to perform well. Those with a task orientation, on the other hand, may more easily achieve recognition and esteem from peers without focusing on it at all.

You may not feel like you're really motivated in this way, but have you ever felt better about your performance only after someone else told you how good it was? Have you ever told yourself that success (yours or others) came down to dumb luck, or else innate intelligence or ability (and not hard work)? If so, you may be more ego oriented than it first seems. Striving to be better than others, to have the "right" approach, equipment or technique, to feel overly confident and be a "winner" are all relatively harmless, but when these feelings are the sole motivation behind achieving a goal, problems can arise. Unlike the task-oriented person, the ego-oriented person will be less able to tolerate rejection or criticism, even if it could improve their performance. They're less likely to enjoy the process overall and may end up rushing tasks, avoiding them all together or—you guessed it—procrastinating.

Consider a generic workplace. Management may set goals for employees, and encourage them to achieve and perform to their highest potential. These goals keep everyone motivated and inspire people to be consistent, work hard, and get results. On a team, someone may be especially ego oriented. Feeling generally insecure in their skills, they may internalize their goals as, "I have to beat everyone else on this team."

This attitude may be seen by a manager as just the right kind of go-getting, ruthless outlook that gets stuff done around the office, but this employee may not actually perform any better. Because this employee has so wrapped up his ego and self-concept in his performance, he's set up a dangerous condition: he finds failure unacceptable. Mistakes are not permitted. He now sees his teammates, in effect, as his enemies rather than his collaborators. So, rather than acting from inspiration, spontaneity, the love of his work or even from a sense of duty, he begins to act out of fear.

With time, this employee may prove himself to be a liability rather than an asset. He may inadvertently steal credit for others' work (since the main aim is to *win*, not to actually master the task within himself), interpret any feedback as a personal attack, and lose all motivation when he isn't at the very top. He may work poorly with others or procrastinate (wouldn't you, if you had placed so much pressure on yourself?). The problem with this employee is that he isn't focused on what matters.

Another employee, however, may have a completely different orientation, and concentrate on the task, not himself.

Completely opposite to the employee who seemed to have a gung-ho, "winner takes all" attitude, this person actually gets the work done—and probably enjoys the process a lot more! He acts from wanting to understand what's in front of him, from the desire to gain competence with increased practice, and from a high tolerance for struggle and occasional failure. He doesn't care too much about failure, since it doesn't reflect on him personally. He merely carries on to find out what *will* work.

This means he's receptive to feedback and criticism (it's great, in his opinion, because now he can understand the problem better) and will actively work with others. Why wouldn't he collaborate, since the more expertise involved, the sooner solutions can be found. He is not threatened by others' success, and can derive satisfaction from the entire process of learning and working—not just the end point. Throughout the process his sense of self-worth is scarcely involved—he feels good about himself whenever he works hard, period. He disentangles himself from competition and end goals and focuses instead on the work in the moment. Which is precisely why he's ultimately far more productive than his ego-driven colleague.

Task orientation is something that can be developed within yourself, or it can be fostered in various situations like workplaces. If you find yourself petrified of failure, uninspired or prone to procrastination, check to see if you can reorient yourself to what's important: gaining mastery of the task. A great tip is to set small, daily goals that focus on the *process* of the work, rather than the *outcome*. So, tell yourself that you want to commit to jogging for twenty minutes every day, rather than that you want to lose ten pounds (and perhaps have everyone admire you for the achievement). The former can be achieved and celebrated every time you put the effort in. It's about the *work*, not about how you'll feel in some projected future.

Wherever you are feeling uninspired in life, take a close look and see if an ego perspective of your goal has caused you to forget the joy of actually mastering this task. Perfectionism is a classic sign of ego orientation. Can you instead commit to doing the messy, sometimes unpredictable work and focus less on how your performance looks to others? Finally, when it comes to procrastination, examine carefully and ask if delaying a task is actually protecting your ego somehow. Many people unconsciously resist the end of a task because they fear being judged, and found wanting. If this is you, try to set those fears aside for the moment and remind yourself that little steps are valuable, that with effort you can improve little by little, and if you're patient you can achieve the best thing of all: the satisfaction of knowing that, on your own terms, you have developed and grown.

Takeaways and action steps:

- Procrastination has been around far longer than you or I have. The term "procrastination" was derived from the Latin words *pro*, meaning "forward,

forth, or in favor of," and *crastinus*, meaning "of tomorrow." In everyday terms, it's when you put off something unpleasant, usually in pursuit of something more enjoyable.
- The pleasure principle is important to understand in the context of procrastination. Our brains have a constant civil war brewing inside; the impulsive and largely subconscious lizard brain wants immediate pleasure at the expense of the slower prefrontal cortex, which makes rational decisions. The prefrontal cortex makes the unpopular choices procrastination is not a fan of, while the lizard brain makes decisions that lead to dopamine and adrenaline being produced. It may seem like a losing battle, but the key to combatting procrastination is being able to regulate our impulses and drives—though not suppress them.
- It's been found that there are nine specific traits associated with procrastination, and these are what we must attempt to pay attention to. They include: (1) inhibition, (2) self-

monitoring, (3) planning and organization, (4) activity shifting, (5) task initiation, (6) task monitoring, (7) emotional control, (8) working memory, and (9) general orderliness. Generally, deficiencies in any of these nine traits will make an individual more susceptible to procrastination. To beat procrastination, we must perform one of the hardest tasks of all: thinking about one's own thinking.

  - Action step: Go through the definitions and examples of each of these nine traits. For each trait, give yourself a score out of 10, where 10 is the highest and 1 is the lowest, for a possible total score of 90. The higher the score, the more prone to procrastination you are. So, score yourself honestly and see how you fare according to the science of it all. Your weak areas will be what you must pay special attention to and attempt to improve upon.
- Many of us will inevitably fall prey to ego orientation, which is when we are

overly focused on comparisons, outside perceptions, and ultimately what others think about us regarding the performance of a task. Obviously, this is not about the task itself, and lends itself to procrastination because in the end, you'd rather not risk embarrassment or judgment. And so you don't move; you are running to stand still. We should instead shift our focus and goals to task orientation, which is the performance of the act itself. It sounds simplistic, but the obstacle is that we are all wired to emotionally protect ourselves, and we will do this subconsciously. You may indeed be acting (or not acting) out of ego orientation, or another type of psychological defense mechanism. Sometimes we don't take action because we don't know how to focus our energy, but other times, we remain stagnant out of fear or avoidance.

Cheat Sheet

Chapter 1. Stop Overthinking

- Overthinking is exactly what you want to avoid in your quest to take action. You truly cannot think and do at the same time, so no matter how productive your mental machinations feel, just know that 99.99 percent of the time, they are holding you back from what you should be doing.

- Overthinking is when your brain is too active with too much information. This is when you should employ the Ostrich Theory and willful ignorance to your benefit. Ostriches, of course, have been mythologized to bury their heads in the sand to avoid danger. Likewise, humans similarly ignore information to avoid danger. Use this to your advantage for once and practice restricting your flow of information and inquiries to become willfully ignorant so you can focus on action rather than thinking.

- o Action step: Limit the amount of information you take in. However many sources you typically consult, cut them in half. Put a cap on your research and rumination time. Practice willful ignorance and realize that not everything is important or urgent. Try to ignore negative indicators based on immediacy, source, category, or diminishing returns.

- A premortem analysis is when you analyze the potential causes of failure before you take action. How is this helpful? Because it makes you focus on one of the few important factors in action—failure—instead of spinning your wheels over other irrelevant aspects.

  - o Action step: Perform a premortem analysis! But make sure that you don't just add this train of thought to your mental to-do list; it should *replace* the other topics you think about. Work backwards from your normal train of thought: ask yourself how potential failures will occur, what the likely causes are, and what solutions you can implement. Chances are most of your mental chatter is not focused in this most important direction.

- A don't-do list is predicated on the fact that most of us know what we should be doing—we are usually just avoiding it or procrastinating. However, most of us get stuck in overthinking because we don't know what we *shouldn't* be doing. This list takes care of that and articulates three types of tasks for you to avoid. You may find that after eliminating these distractions, you'll be left with a clear path for what to take action on.

    o Action step: Create your don't-do list. Make it as long and detailed as possible with the tasks that have diminishing returns, are waiting on other people, and don't add value to your goals. Have the intention of knowing exactly what to focus on after you're done.

- One of the biggest reasons we overthink? Uncertainty in the outcome, which is related to insecurity and fear. We want to be thorough to the point that we know we will not fail if we act. Unfortunately, that's impossible, and if you attempt it you're just going to stay on the sidelines, searching for something that doesn't exist. Uncertainty to most of us is nearly synonymous with negativity, but that's not the reality. Uncertainty is omnipresent in everything we do, and it is actually freeing to change your expectations. Once you accept uncertainty, you'll be willing to risk a little more and take to action a bit quicker.

    o Action step: Think about the ways you already accept uncertainty in your life. In fact, compose a short list and rate the relative probabilities and levels of danger. You could be hit with a car every time you cross the road.

Eventually, when you accept that fact, it just fades into background static. Remember this when you are faced with something potentially nerve-wracking or fearful.

Chapter 2. Err on the Side of Action

- What does it mean to err on the side of action? Simply, it means that instead of freezing or analyzing, you should attempt to make your default response action. Have an action bias.
- The first way to err on the side of action is to break through what's known as comfortable inaction. This is where you feel that things are good enough, so you might as well not disrupt the status quo. This is where we get sayings like "good is the enemy of great" and so on, but it's true—you will never live the way you want if you are too comfortable where you are now.
    - Action step: You aren't uncomfortable enough to take action, so increase the amount of discomfort that comes along with

inaction so you have no choice but to act. For something you are trying to break past a plateau on, allow your imagination to run wild on the various negative consequences you will face. Think about the rewards you will miss. Think about the short and long-term repercussions. Once these seem more urgent and tangible, action will be far easier.

- It's tough to get started when you're facing something huge. You already dread it because you know it will not feel rewarding and you won't be able to finish anytime soon. That in itself is discouraging. Therefore, break up your tasks into as tiny steps as possible, steps so small that it's almost no different from your status quo of inaction.
    - Action step: Break down a task you've been dreading into ten small, individual steps. Can you break it down into fifteen, and then twenty? How does it feel to achieve something, no matter how small? I bet it feels great.

- The 40-70 Rule popularized by Colin Powell states that you should get started with no less than 40 percent of the information you feel is necessary, but no more than 70 percent. For our purposes, focus on getting started with 40 percent—what might feel like an insufficient amount of information. But in reality, you've already hit the point of diminishing returns, and anything else will be learned more effectively along the way.
    - Action step: Apply the 40-70 Rule to elements other than information: confidence, planning, learning, and preparing. Write down the top ten details you need to complete something. Now try eliminating three of those details. Did it make a difference? For that matter, how many of the ten do you actually need to get started? To simply begin, you likely need nowhere close to ten.
- Indecision is basically overthinking by another name, and it is an equivalent obstacle to erring on the side of action

and gaining momentum. Indecision is defeatable in many ways, with the common thread between many of the methods being some sort of pickiness.
  - Action step: Attempt to apply all the tactics described to something you are having trouble deciding on. These include: commit with the intent of backtracking, apply strict boundaries, utilize a default choice, seek satisfactory choices over perfect ones, engage in intentionally judgmental thinking, and be purposefully general and vague. Which one works best for you and helps you reach a decision the quickest?
- Finally, you can limit your information consumption. Very little of what we consume is helpful or even relevant. Most of it is also consumed unconsciously, without us realizing that we are spending so much time and effort on it—we get sucked in. Cultivate self-awareness, curate your consumption and reduce your media sources so you

can devote your limited energy toward work and motion.
- o Action step: make a list of what you consume for a week, and make a resolution to cut down on at least 50 percent of it. Preview information before you engage with it, and view everything as a pitch for your time and energy.

Chapter 3. The Take-Action Mindset

- As you can tell, taking action is more than something you simply decide to do one day. It's a habit, and ideally will become part of the mindset with which you approach the world.
- One way to get into this mindset is to approach it from a different angle. Instead of constantly working to take action, you could seek to banish zero days from your life. A zero day is simply a day (or other time period) in which you take no action toward your goals. You just need to be able to say yes or no for a time period to avoid your zero day, and it can be as small an action as you

can think of. The point is to build consistency and eventual motivation.

- o Action step: Set up your zero days. Set a specific goal, and promise to do something tangible to further that goal. It doesn't matter how small it is; just make it so no day goes by resulting in zero action. Try to have a string of unbroken days.

- Do you find yourself focused on solutions or problems? As we have often said, you can't think and do at the same time. When you're concentrating on problems, you're stuck in place and not interested in moving forward. When you're focused on solutions, you're asking the right questions and jumping into motion. If you want to get from Point A to Point B, there is very little room for problem-focused thinking.
  - o Action step: Stop asking why. Why doesn't particularly help you formulate a plan to move forward and take action. Instead of fixating on

something that is already a fact you can't change, ask yourself questions centered around what you can do first and what you can do now.
- Do you pat yourself on the back just for thinking about taking action? A big pitfall is when intentions and actions blur together. This causes you to be fooled into thinking you've done what you're supposed to do, even though you've done nothing but spin your wheels. Separate these two distinct acts and learn to not feel so satisfied from mere intentions.
    - Action step: Whenever you realize you are starting to blur the gap between intentions and actions, think in terms of plans. Take your intention and break it down into four small steps that will make the intention reality. It's important to build a mental separation between these two elements.
- Finally, learn to distinguish between urgent and important tasks. One

matters, while the other only appears to because it may have more time constraints. But urgency by itself doesn't denote any kind of priority. To master the difference, try using the Eisenhower Matrix to divide your tasks into four separate categories; you'll find that much less matters than you previously thought. It is similar to the don't-do list because it can create clarity on what you are wasting your time on.

- o Action step: Create an Eisenhower Matrix. Understand what needs to be done, what can be skipped, and what should be eliminated immediately.

Chapter 4. Maximize Momentum

- One of the best ways to gain and keep momentum is to deal with your excuses. I'm sorry to break it to you, but almost all of them are fake. They are either intentional or unconscious lies. The main culprits are: "I'm not good enough," "I don't know where to start," and "now is not the right time."
  - Action step: For something you are trying to avoid right now, list out a few excuses. Are they real excuses, or are they just explanations for why something is difficult? There is a very large difference between the two.
- Temptation bundling is the act of blending instant gratification (inaction) and delayed gratification (action). Basically, you bribe yourself by pairing action with rewards—that way, both the current you and the future you are satisfied.

- - Action step: Create a list of the actions you have been avoiding, and add a list of bribes or rewards that you can tie to each action. For instance, practicing the piano gets you a piece of chocolate. Create your own pairings to experience the benefits of temptation bundling.
- Your environment might be one of the most underappreciated aspects of changing your behaviors and mindset. The human brain operates on what it sees and what surrounds it, so you must curate your environment to help you be action-oriented. You can do this by making the easy thing the right thing. Think about how you can remove your willpower from the equation.
  - Action step: Take at least three steps in curating your environment to make taking action almost effortless. This can be putting things into your path, removing distractions, or

even placing reminders everywhere.
- The if-then technique is a way of chaining behaviors together. You link a normal, everyday behavior with a goal-oriented action. This sounds fancy, but you are just trying to create a habit out of something unpleasurable. The magic is in the pre-decision and making a rule for yourself before you must make a decision.
    - Action step: Just like with temptation bundling, list out a set of everyday behaviors, such as brushing teeth, and create a separate list of actions that move you toward your goal. Pair them so that every time your everyday activity occurs, you take action toward your goal.
- Multitasking is a big, fat myth. You probably have the best of intentions with it—after all, multitasking is an excess of action. But too much action will sadly leave you with no action, as you won't be able to focus and truly

progress. The key to beating this is single-tasking and 100 percent concentration and commitment to one task at a time.

- o Action step: Realize that modern multitasking is actually switching between tasks in a short amount of time. This doesn't work well because of attention residue. So go to your calendar or planner and block off larger amounts of time devoted to one task only. Have a distraction list ready to jot down thoughts that would otherwise derail you during your single-tasking session. Understand that even without constant attention, the world outside of your task will not fall apart.

- The Pomodoro Technique helps keep you on track and on task, rather than getting you up from ground zero. A pomodoro consists of twenty-five minutes of focused, uninterrupted work, followed by five minutes break. Rinse and repeat as many cycles as you can. It's possible to build up to intervals of fifty minutes and ten minutes, or even sixty minutes, sixty minutes, and then thirty minutes for a break.

- o Action step: Do this now. Not much else to say about this one.

Chapter 5. Beating Procrastination

- Procrastination has been around far longer than you or I have. The term "procrastination" was derived from the Latin words *pro*, meaning "forward, forth, or in favor of," and *crastinus*, meaning "of tomorrow." In everyday terms, it's when you put off something unpleasant, usually in pursuit of something more enjoyable.
- The pleasure principle is important to understand in the context of procrastination. Our brains have a constant civil war brewing inside; the impulsive and largely subconscious lizard brain wants immediate pleasure at the expense of the slower prefrontal

cortex, which makes rational decisions. The prefrontal cortex makes the unpopular choices procrastination is not a fan of, while the lizard brain makes decisions that lead to dopamine and adrenaline being produced. It may seem like a losing battle, but the key to combatting procrastination is being able to regulate our impulses and drives—though not suppress them.

- It's been found that there are nine specific traits associated with procrastination, and these are what we must attempt to pay attention to. They include: (1) inhibition, (2) self-monitoring, (3) planning and organization, (4) activity shifting, (5) task initiation, (6) task monitoring, (7) emotional control, (8) working memory, and (9) general orderliness. Generally, deficiencies in any of these nine traits will make an individual more susceptible to procrastination. To beat procrastination, we must perform one of the hardest tasks of all: thinking about one's own thinking.

- Action step: Go through the definitions and examples of each of these nine traits. For each trait, give yourself a score out of 10, where 10 is the highest and 1 is the lowest, for a possible total score of 90. The higher the score, the more prone to procrastination you are. So, score yourself honestly and see how you fare according to the science of it all. Your weak areas will be what you must pay special attention to and attempt to improve upon.
- Many of us will inevitably fall prey to ego orientation, which is when we are overly focused on comparisons, outside perceptions, and ultimately what others think about us regarding the performance of a task. Obviously, this is not about the task itself, and lends itself to procrastination because in the end, you'd rather not risk embarrassment or judgment. And so you don't move; you are running to stand still. We should instead shift our focus and goals to task orientation, which is the performance of

the act itself. It sounds simplistic, but the obstacle is that we are all wired to emotionally protect ourselves, and we will do this subconsciously. You may indeed be acting (or not acting) out of ego orientation, or another type of psychological defense mechanism. Sometimes we don't take action because we don't know how to focus our energy, but other times, we remain stagnant out of fear or avoidance.

www.ingramcontent.com/pod-product-compliance
Lightning Source LLC
Chambersburg PA
CBHW071158070526
44584CB00019B/2845